BANDONEON
WORKING WITH PINA BAUSCH

Raimund Hoghe / Ulli Weiss

BANDONEON
WORKING WITH PINA BAUSCH

Translated by Penny Black

With an Introduction by Katalin Trencsényi

Edited by Katalin Trencsényi

OBERON BOOKS
LONDON

WWW.OBERONBOOKS.COM

First published in the English language in 2016 by Oberon Books Ltd
521 Caledonian Road, London N7 9RH
Tel: +44 (0) 20 7607 3637 / Fax: +44 (0) 20 7607 3629
e-mail: info@oberonbooks.com
www.oberonbooks.com

Cover photo: Dominique Mercy performing in *Bandoneon* (1980).
Photography: Ulli Weiss.

CONTENTS

INTRODUCTION

What is the point of Bandoneon?

by Katalin Trencsényi

"Reality no longer has just one meaning or reading. Entire worlds exist beneath or behind our perceptions."

– Marianne Van Kerkhoven

"If things are not carefully and very cautiously covered – they will never be discovered."

– Federico García Lorca

Art becomes commercial at precisely the moment when its time is past. The tension between success and impact, which Brecht spoke of, is important in this respect: that one is always overtaken by success before a real impact can occur. As long as a thing works it is not successful, and when success is there then the impact is over. This is because there can only be an impact if, as for example in the theatre, the audience is split, brought home to its real situation. But that means there will be no agreement, no success. Success happens when everybody is cheering, in other words, when there is nothing more to say.[1]

These words of playwright Heiner Müller illuminate the dilemma performance-makers face. Their aim is to connect with the audience, and through the window of this temporary connection to enter into a conversation. They raise questions about society or the human condition, and encourage spectators to jolt out of their habitual thinking and examine their lives from a different perspective.

However, there is a risk of an adverse reaction from the spectator if the reflection in the 'mirror of the performance' is unflattering. Understanding a new artistic language can be challenging, and it might take a long time before audiences learn to 'read' with confidence a new type of performance.

Yet, once this language is well established, there is a potential danger that this newfound means of expression may become shorthand, a commodity that is expected from the artist again and again until it becomes an empty form, devoid of its power to change us. Once the impact is lost, art becomes a profitably marketable product, with little risk and much commercial success.

* * *

Pina Bausch's artistic search for her own expressive language in dance started at a time when the global landscape of contemporary dance was changing. In post-war America and Germany artists were turning away from strong formal techniques, and instead searching for 'alternative dance experiences and performing styles'.[2] In New York, where Bausch herself had spent some defining years, the scene was bubbling. Artists at the Judson Church in the 1960s were experimenting with the aim of establishing a 'radically new economy of movement'.[3] American art critic Annette Michelson explains:

> This required a systematic critique of the rhetoric, conventions, the aesthetic hierarchies imposed by traditional or classical dance forms. That rhetoric was, in fact, reversed, destroyed, in what came to be known as the dance of 'ordinary language' and of 'task performance'.[4]

These tasks served a double strategy, according to theorist Rosalind E. Krauss: 'to exchange illusionism for real-time and to de-psychologise the performer'.[5]

Bausch, herself, was going in a similar direction. She had an open-minded, 'holistic' approach to dance, embracing other art forms; and 'a certain honesty'[6] that she had learnt from Kurt Jooss and other masters at the Folkwangschule (1955-59), 'where all the arts were gathered under one roof' and 'many joint projects came into being'.[7] She had absorbed the techniques and the experimental spirit of the American contemporary dance, and discovered her determination during her 'years of apprenticeship' (1959-62) – studying with José Limón and Antony Tudor at the Juilliard School in New York, and working with other innovative artists such as Paul Taylor, Paul Sanasardo and Donya Feuer. At the Folkwang Ballet (1962-68) Bausch began the search for her own forms of expression as a dancer and choreographer. As she later noted:

> To express what really lay in my heart, it was impossible for me to use other people's material and forms of movement. Simply out of respect. What I had seen and learnt was taboo for me. I put myself in the difficult situation: why and how can I express something?[8]

Bausch's sense of responsibility and love of work, demonstrated during her directorship (1969–73) of the Folkwang Ballet were other essential qualities for this quest. With her appointment as Director of Dance for the Wuppertaler Bühnen in 1973 (thanks to the support and persistence of the visionary intendant, Arno Wüstenhöfer), Bausch became the first female dancer with modern training to be given a leading position in the post-war German theatre establishment.

Wuppertal, a melancholic and somewhat faded town, stretching along the narrow valley of the Wupper River, enclosed by steep hillsides and greenery, had seen better days in the late nineteenth and early twentieth century with its thriving textile industry. Its steel and concrete architecture today retains traces of that confident and prosperous past that allowed this small town to dream big. Some of these bourgeois houses (including the former home of Friedrich Engels), with pointed roofs, painted window frames and wooden shutters, still testify to the former glories, while the retro-futuristic monorail that winds above the river, the Town Hall and the Opera House show the grand hopes which this sleepy town once had about its future.

Having lost the majority of its coal-based industry in the latter part of the twentieth century, Wuppertal still holds onto the dream of being an important place for contemporary culture. Its Sculpture Park, the University of Wuppertal and the more recent plans for an International Dance Centre illustrate the dream this provincial town is chasing: to be relevant and important, and not to be overshadowed by its internationally vibrant and culturally alluring neighbours, Düsseldorf and Cologne.

Yet, at the edge of the old market square, near the station of the Schwebebahn, still stands the concrete building of the Lichtburg, the disused cinema, as it did in the 1970s, arid and well-worn, preserving something of the feeling of the place where Pina Bausch used to rehearse with the Tanztheater Wuppertal.

When she began her job in Wuppertal as Director of Dance for the Wuppertaler Bühnen, Bausch took on responsibility for three stages, a traditional troupe of ballet dancers, and sometimes had to work with an orchestra and a chorus. Her predecessor, choreographer Ivan Sertić, who cultivated a classical ballet repertoire, had been very popular with the audience. Bausch was aware of that: 'A certain type of aesthetic was expected; there was no disputing that there were other forms of beauty apart from this.'[9]

However, Bausch (who had already shed her ballet dancer's years, including dancing for the Metropolitan Opera in New York) had different ideas about what it meant to dance: 'I believe that you have to learn to dance anew, or you need to learn something different, then maybe you can dance again.'[10] – as she later summed it up. This aspiration for 'reconceiving the medium of dance',[11] was not a programme or theory she envisioned and decided to realise, it was rather a process of acting upon an instinct, listening to an inner voice, which led to a journey, a quest into the unknown: 'I had to decide: do I follow a plan or do I get involved with something which I don't know where it will take me.'[12]

What was clear from the outset, though, was that whatever would be presented in Wuppertal under Bausch, the genre 'classical ballet' would not be flexible enough to cover it. To signify this shift and help the audience understand what to expect, Bausch changed the name of the ensemble to Tanztheater: 'Before I arrived there was the Wuppertaler Ballet, and ballet is tied into classical dance. The term 'dance theatre' is very comprehensive but is not necessarily connected to classical ballet. That was very important to me.'[13]

This name change also indicated the movement with which Bausch intended to link her work: namely the German expressionist tradition, the work of Rudolf Laban, Mary Wigman and Kurt Jooss. So Bausch began moving away from the formal language of the classical ballet in order to find a free expression that would reflect her and her dancers' own personal experiences.

For this endeavour Bausch needed an ensemble of dancers with different qualities from those a classical ballet troupe could offer. She kept only one solo dancer from her predecessor's original company, Jan Minarik (who became one of the core figures of Bausch's ensemble), and recruited new artists from the Folkwang Ballet as well as from abroad. Amongst the new dancers she invited was Dominique Mercy, a key artist of the Tanztheater, with whom she developed a deep, life-long friendship, and for whom she created several important roles.

A glance at the Bausch-harvested dancers of the Wuppertal Tanztheater, 'with an astounding range of physiques, types, sizes, personalities',[14] reveals that this was not 'a typical troupe of flawless ballet drones',[15] but an ensemble full of characters, specially chosen and developed for expressive dance.[16] As Bausch later reflected:

> Whom can I work with after all? With such people who have inner things that are unknown for me, even if these things are alien to me. It interests me less when I know what to expect from someone.[17]

First Bausch experimented with using dancers and singers together on the stage, in a new genre she called dance-opera, and created *Iphigenie auf Tauris* (1974), and *Orpheus und Eurydike* (1975). In this latter choreography she doubled the roles: each character was played by a singer and a dancer; achieving a powerful unity of music, singing and dance on the stage. We can only guess where this kind of Gesamtkunstwerk aesthetics might have led, combining the orchestra, the chorus and the dancers in search for new expression. But since their relationship didn't prove harmonious, Bausch gradually stopped working with the theatre's orchestra and chorus, and began to use recorded music with the dancers instead.

Abandoning live music brought about an opportunity: the orchestra pit became redundant, thus giving the possibility of extending the stage over it, providing a bigger area for the dancers to use. This expansion of the space for dance could be regarded as a symbolic act: the emancipation of the dancer. It also reveals Bausch's interpretation of the relationship between dance and music: emphasising dance as gesture as opposed to dance as an illustration of music.

The choice to use recorded music on the stage altered the traditional hierarchy of music and dance. Dance did not equal movements set to an already written piece of music, choreographed on the body of a dancer, but an independent form of expression, for which the gestures were to be found within the personality of the individual dancer. These found movements were then further accentuated by being paired up with a fitting (or contrasting) piece of music.

This partnership between music and gesture remained a characteristic feature of Bausch's work. As Dominique Mercy explained, the movements were usually developed without music[18] – the gestures' main inspiration being the dancers' individual responses to Bausch's 'mobilising questions'. Norbert Servos, specialist in dance theatre confirms: 'The dances and scenes almost always emerged independently of the music, thus developing and affirming their self-sufficiency – amongst other things.'[19]

Musical segments were found in parallel to this process, and added to the action at a later stage of the work, often taking advantage of the friction between sound and gesture.[20]

The technical opportunities of using recorded music on stage were further explored in *Blaubart...* (1977), in which a tape recorder on wheels (attached to a long extension cable hanging from the ceiling) became a chief element of the design (created by Rolf Borzik). In fact, this was the actual tape deck on which Bartók's music was played. Stopping the music, rewinding the tape on the stage and revisiting the same musical motif again and again enabled the protagonist (performed by Jan Minarik) 'to wind forwards and backwards to examine his life'.[21]

Rewinding the music on the stage also broke up the flow of the choreography and served as a Brechtian V-effect: jolting the spectators out of being carried away by the representation on the stage, and bringing them back to the immediacy of the piece. At the same time, the repetition of these dance sequences served as an incessant invitation for reflection and re-examination of the audience's own male-female relationships.

Having the tape recorder operated on the stage by the dancer, like a master of ceremonies, highlighted Bausch's statement that the agent for the dance was the dancer: he orchestrated what was happening on the stage.

The use of recorded music opened up further possibilities for Bausch: to work with a variety of musical genres, from classical, folk, jazz or pop (even within one dance piece), and to cross the boundaries between 'serious' and popular music. In this way Bausch could shape the musical landscape for her pieces. From 1977 onwards she moved from a longer piece by a single composer to an increasingly eclectic collage of songs and music. This musical collage technique corresponded to the collage dramaturgy of Bausch's choreography.

Bausch found a great musical collaborator in Mathias Burkert, who since 1980 helped her with research (to find music) and composition (to shape the musical dramaturgy of the pieces), 'developing dramatic tension and attuning the music precisely to the dances and scenes'.[22]

* * *

The sets for Bausch's choreographies were designed by her long-term collaborators, first by her partner, Rolf Borzik (1944-80), and after his untimely death, by Peter Pabst (b.1944). Both designers worked with Bausch throughout the development process in an intensive collaboration, attending rehearsals and developing the set simultaneously as the piece grew in the rehearsal room.

Bausch had a very strong relationship with her designers. This is how she recalls her work with Borzik:

> The collaboration was very intense. We were a source of mutual inspiration for each other. Anything that came up whilst we were creating a new piece: questions, endeavours, doubts, even moments of despair – we knew we could rely on each other. Rolf Borzik was always present during rehearsals. He was always there. He always supported and protected me. And his imagination was boundless.[23]

Bausch's friendship with Pabst dates back to the late 1970s, when the director of the Schauspielhaus Bochum (one of the most prominent theatres in Germany), Peter Zadek, a supporter of Bausch's work, introduced the two artists to each other. Bausch, in her Kyoto Prize award ceremony speech, remembered their work fondly:

> Peter Pabst and I have been involved with great pleasure in the adventure of doing a piece that doesn't exist yet. But that is not all. For me Peter Pabst is not only important as a set designer, but through his advice and actions, for us all and for the many concerns of the dance theatre, he has become indispensable. (…) He and my dancers have accompanied myself on such a long and difficult path and continue to go with me in great trust, for that I am very grateful.[24]

The design for the Tanztheater Wuppertal's dance pieces matched the comprehensive aesthetics and purposefulness of Bausch's choreographies: that 'everything has a meaning, everything must be essential to the unfolding of the performance'.[25] The design was not representational; rather it was poetic, playful, surprising and flexible: balanced between reality and a psychological, imagined, dream-like reality. The design was 'open' enough to leave room for the dancers' movements and the spectators' imagination to 'inhabit' it, thus accommodating multiple interpretations. It also contained the 'this is what it is here and now, no more, no less' feeling of performance art, preserving a quintessence of reality and the feeling of spontaneity.

Borzik called his designs 'free action rooms, which make us into happy and cruel children'.[26] Pabst called them 'frames' as opposed to a completed picture.[27] Both designers' descriptions refer to a set that enables and requires the dancers to be creative and inventive. These sets also had the possibility for transformation (often by the movements of the dancers), such as the field of carnations in *Nelken* (1982) that during the performance is gradually trampled over and destroyed.

The designs themselves were daring and innovative. According to Bausch, Borzik was the first set designer 'who brought nature onto the stage – soil covered the floor of the stage in *The Rite of Spring*; leaves for *Bluebeard*, undergrowth and brushwood for *Come Dance With Me*[28] and finally water for *Arien*'.[29]

Borzik's and Pabst's use of natural elements on the stage contrasted and challenged the illusions dance (and especially classical ballet) strives to maintain: that the bodies in the air are weightless, and the movements (lifts and jumps) that seemingly defy gravity are effortless. Instead, the design emphasised the dancers' efforts and re-introduced the struggle against gravity in the dance by creating obstacles for the dancers to move in or through, and surfaces that don't spring, or where the dancers' feet leave a mark or can even slip. As reviewer Randolin Zinn noted, the spectators are meant to see the dancers' sweat and hear their heavy breathing.[30]

This natural layer or obstacles on the floor made dancing look an effort, an artistic expression that had to be realised in spite of or against the set. For instance, dancing through a stage covered with chairs in *Café Müller* (1978).[31] At times it made the act of dancing daring or dangerous (for instance, dancing on a swimming island in *Ein Trauerspiel* (1994), as well as changed the quality of the movement when water (*Arien* (1979), peat (*Le Sacre du printemps* (1975), or turf (*1980, a piece of Pina Bausch* (1980)) was covering the dance floor.

Notably, though, for Bausch these elements of nature did not mean obstruction; rather the opposite: a positive, sensuous experience:

> It's a big joy to dance in the earth. (…) If you walk on the grass, it's silent, it's soft, or there are some mosquitoes around. It has a smell. It has a certain temperature… Or when you are in the water, when you run, there is the noise of it, or if it's quiet, it's like a mirror… Or the leaves when you walk…you can see where you walked. It's joining with something. For me it's not a resistance. It's the opposite. It's touching.[32]

Dancer Julie Shanahan spoke about the experience of dancing on the turf:

> When we rehearse, everything is loud because you're walking with high heels. But with the grass on stage, there's a quietness just like with snow. And the beauty of the green comes out – you see it on a stage and suddenly grass looks completely amazing. That's what Pina did: she made you look at simple everyday things and realise that they are beautiful.[33]

For Bausch the concept of the set was inseparable from her overall aesthetic:

> Many things we do on stage are real; people run, they fall, they smash themselves against the walls, or they are soaked in water. The grass on stage really smells. The contract between the public – it is all real. That is what I like. If we experience a moment together in the theatre, it is very realistic, and that for me is hope, because it is something real.[34]

As well as the introduction of reality to the design, Pabst also explains how he and Bausch played with the limitations of the traditional Guckkastenbühne: 'I love the end-on staging, because many things gain life there from the contradiction that an inappropriate object was placed in the space.'[35] This imminent deconstruction built into the design to prevent the feeling of 'completeness' added a layer of grotesque, irony and sometimes self-mockery to the visuals of the piece. One only needs to think of the Borzik-designed enormous hippopotamus, that featured in *Arien*, or a crocodile eating a ballerina in *Keuschheitslegende* (1979). Sometimes surprising proportions achieved this feeling of the absurd, for instance the way the walls of the ballroom for the tea dance in *Kontakthof* (1978) dwarfed the dancers, or the giant cactii forest Pabst created for *Ahnen* (1987).

Bausch and her designers played with the theatrical conventions to their limits. For instance, when the curtain rose for *Palermo Palermo* (1989), the audience was presented with a brick wall that totally blocked the stage: the symbolic 'fourth wall' here literally appeared. After a long silence the wall collapsed and allowed the dancers to stumble through the rubble, to break out from the 'theatrical' into the real.

* * *

'I am not interested in how people move but what moves them.' [36] – asserted Bausch in several interviews. One might say that her life's work was observing people, and this attention and examination fed all her works. 'Bausch's themes are positively Strindbergian', noted *The Guardian*'s dance critic, John O'Mahony, 'loss, loneliness, grief, death, leave-taking and the tortuous relations between the sexes. But there is also wicked humour too.'[37] This (often absurd) humour and irony are the tools Bausch used to avoid sentimentalism and pathos in her works.

During her first five years in Wuppertal (1973–78), Bausch's choreographies were often based on archetypal stories that depicted relationships between man and woman: *Iphigenie auf Tauris* (1974), *Orpheus und Eurydike* (1975), *Le Sacre du printemps* (1975), *Blaubart – Beim Anhören einer Tonbandaufnahme von Béla Bartóks Oper "Herzog Blaubarts Burg"* (1977), and *Er nimmt sie an die Hand und führt sie in das Schloß, die anderen folgen (Macbeth-Projekt)* (1978). She showed the eternal fight between the sexes in its vulnerability and ugliness, interpreting relationships in an uncompromising, raw, sometimes brutally honest way, while deconstructing the conventional, formal language of ballet.

However, both *Blaubart...* and the *Macbeth-Projekt* are already departures from the narrative. In both pieces the original plot is used rather as a framework, a starting point for associations on the topic; and instead of unfolding the story, the choreography wanders on an inner landscape of human emotions. Nonetheless, this 'wandering' is realised through a meticulously constructed form, using very simple but effective tools (repetition, contrast etc.).

'Dance is not instinctual, on the contrary: it is very much a conscious affair,'[38] said Bausch. A careful analysis of her compositions shows how strong Bausch's sense of form was. The unique building blocks of each piece were placed together to create the composition with the greatest concern and attention to the minutest detail. What may look chaotic or random at first is in fact precisely engineered, using non-linear composition and layering. Yet Bausch avoids the obvious in her dramaturgy; she prefers hiding to revealing, and often loosens the structure of the work in order to avoid too neat and completed a shape. The structure of Bausch's choreographies demonstrates her artistic refusal to impose (or acknowledge) a universal order or a viewpoint from which one can overlook and comprehend the whole world. On the contrary, in her choreographies, Bausch often leaves a door open to the unknown.

By the late 1970s the traditional dichotomy between the soloist (whose journey is the theme of the piece) and the chorus (in the background during the protagonist's journey) had disappeared from Bausch's choreography. Whereas this division of the dancers can still be observed in *Le Sacre du printemps*, and *Orpheus...*, and to some extent even in *Blaubart...*; with the disappearance of the narrative from the choreographies, the ensemble, as a collective of individuals, becomes the 'protagonist' of the pieces. This thematic and structural change was a result of Bausch's new working method, where the focus shifted onto the dancers' individual experiences and their responses to certain themes; thus the personality of each and every dancer gained more importance and became intensified in the pieces. Instead of following one character on the stage, the audience sees snippets from many people's lives; and the piece becomes the sum of those individual experiences – almost like an investigation into our collective subconscious.

Another 'reverse' tendency can be observed in Bausch's way of developing the characters for the pieces. In contrast to traditional ballet pieces, where the soloist 'puts on' an existing role, portraying and enriching it with his/her personality, thus giving an indistinguishable character to the role, in Bausch's work the roles are developed the other way round. She begins with the personality of her dancers, their individual experiences, memories, stories, movements etc., and from these responses, bit by bit, she develops the piece and the stage persona (role) for each dancer for the given choreography.

This development technique is akin to the creative processes used in collaborative (devised) theatre – an alternative way of performance-making that sprung to life in the late 1960s and early 1970s. In common with the idea of devised theatre which 'challenges the prevailing ideology of one person's text under one person's direction',[39] instead encouraging 'collective creation of art',[40] Bausch's work relied on and celebrated the creativity of her ensemble.

As a result, the new pieces became more complex, fragmented and layered with multiple stories and memories coming from the dancers. Bausch said:

> There are plenty of things present on the stage, in every minute there are many more signs, many more people than we recognise. Sometimes we have no idea how much is there simultaneously: how many memories, how much time and history…it is good that we can't explain it all.[41]

The new direction in which Bausch was heading with the Tanztheater Wuppertal was not welcomed by the local audience. Dance critic Jochen Schmidt, who had been following her work closely since the 1970s and called Bausch, 'the Mother Courage of new dance'[42] recalls:

> In the theatre, where Bausch used to watch the performances of her pieces in the last row, she was spat on and her hair was pulled. At nights anonymous phone calls woke her up with rude and filthy insults, and demanded she left town.[43]

Bausch, however, was unswerving. From 1978 onwards she discontinued employing even the hint of a narrative as the vehicle of the performance, and instead used a feeling or emotion as the 'leitmotif' for the show (tenderness for *Kontakthof*, loss for *1980*…etc.) which she then investigated from many sides. Yet, she warned that what was presented on the stage was an 'abstraction' and was 'not a private thing'.[44]

'Words don't translate thoughts very well,'[45] remarked Bausch. Similarly, the words that are uttered in a Wuppertal Tanztheater performance don't add up to a coherent textual body; they serve rather as the debris of a civilization: snippets of conversations, quotes, short, insubstantial presentations to the audience, or absurd dialogues. They often convey humour, sometimes by 'promising' to be more important announcements (amplified by a microphone), but in reality are no more than banal, commonplace utterances.

The choreographies time by time employ 'task performances': people performing small, every day activities, like getting dressed, washing themselves, eating or shaving. Bausch often emphasises these moments with contrast or humour. For instance in *Two Cigarettes in the Dark* (1985) Mechthild Großmann, wearing a loose cream evening dress that leaves her breasts exposed, with a cigarette hanging from her mouth carries hay to the stage with a pitchfork.

Postmodern reflections about dance also appear, playing with the different meanings dance has for the audience and the ensemble. Bausch holds a grotesque mirror to the conventions of ballet (classical ballet movements or references to the drill of ballet training often appear in an ironic context), and challenges the expectations of an audience that came to watch a 'proper' dance. This is shown most explicitly in *Nelken*, when a frustrated Dominique Mercy confronts the spectators: 'You want to see something, eh?' And he spins and jumps and travels across the stage, showing off his virtuosity as a classical ballet dancer, performing exquisite 'tour en l'air', 'grand jeté', 'entrechat six', while shouting, 'How many do you want?!', and growing angrier and angrier that the audience wants to see this 'circus' performance instead of the ensemble's work.

Bausch is not even afraid to mock her own method. In *Walzer* (1982), Jan Minarik comes to the microphone at the front of the stage and starts to demonstrate Bausch's famous

23

rehearsal room questions, with help from the rest of the company, thus giving an ironic insight into her process. The scene is irresistibly comic. For instance, to the question, 'What do you associate from King Kong?', the Czech Minarik replies: 'He was a foreigner too.'

In the works of the late 1970s and 1980s, Bausch's strong sense of form remains, but she departs from having one focal point on the stage, and instead uses multiple foci, applying collage technique to assemble the various fragments. It becomes the spectator's choice as to which action on the stage they follow; but they can't see everything, since Bausch only occasionally frames the view. Consequently, the spectator, just like the characters he/she is watching, will have only a partial knowledge of the action on the stage. As the world (on the stage) appears fragmented and incoherent, with multiple actions happening simultaneously, the spectator loses his/her privileged, objective position of moral or intellectual superiority. We know no more than the characters on the stage – and are similarly at a loss in this world.

What is offered, in exchange for the loss of 'universal' meaning, is the multiplicity of interpretations for the spectator. We see ourselves in Bausch's pieces – and understand them individually. As Bausch remarked:

> Each person in the audience is part of the piece in a way; you bring your own experience, your own fantasies, your own feelings in response to what you see. There is something happening inside. You only understand if you let that happen, it's not something you can do with your intellect. So everybody, according to their experience, has a different feeling, a different impression. Also, on different days, what you feel is different.[46]

* * *

A decade in her new post, yet the audience in Wuppertal still could not accept Bausch's work. Dancer Meryl Tankard recalls:

> Sometimes they would throw oranges at us when we were trying to dance. Once a man got up on stage and took a bucket of water I had as a prop and tried to throw it over one of the other dancers who was repeating a poem over and over. But she ducked and the water went all over the audience.[47]

For a long time, the critics were too confused about the value of Bausch's work. During the Tanztheater Wuppertal's first American tours (in June 1984 and September – October 1985) Bausch was called: 'Germany's radical visionary',[48] 'the most talked-about choreographer in Europe',[49] 'a major talent',[50] 'dancing on new ground',[51] and a choreographer who 'redefines dance'.[52] Whereas other reviewers labelled her work 'anti-feminist',[53] 'uncompelling',[54] 'tedious',[55] 'sadomasochistic',[56] 'doesn't amount to much',[57] 'but is it dance?',[58] 'avant-garde chic',[59] 'silly, empty, stupid, self-indulgent, self-congratulatory',[60] and, most famously: 'pornography of pain'.[61]

Around the same time the elite of contemporary art 'began making pilgrimages to Wuppertal, among them those who became avid Bausch supporters – Susan Sontag, Robert Wilson, Peter Brook, Robert Lepage,'[62] Federico Fellini (who called her a 'saint on roller skates'[63]), Alain Platel, Heiner Müller, and novelist Péter Nádas, who, in his essay about her work, called Bausch a 'philosopher of bodies'.[64]

This is exactly the kind of division Heiner Müller referred to in the quote at the beginning of this essay, when 'the audience is split, brought home to its real situation';[65] a discrepancy of opinions that, ideally, generates an animated discourse about the work, forces us to think about its theme and our response to it, and consequently re-examine the world we live in now.

* * *

From the 1980s (first sporadically, then regularly) the Tanztheater Wuppertal began the series of international co-productions, the 'residency pieces',[66] for which the ensemble travelled to a host city, spent a few weeks there in residency, worked in a studio as well as lived and felt the spirit of that place and became acquainted with its people. On return to Wuppertal, a new piece was developed, which (after its Wuppertal premiere) would be taken back to the host city for a short tour, as a gesture of gratitude for the hospitality.

Although the first 'official' residency piece is regarded as *Viktor* (1986), a collaboration with the Teatro Argentina (Teatro di Roma), an earlier piece, *Bandoneon* (1980), can be considered to be the forerunner of these series.[67] The creation of this work was preceded by the ensemble's South American tour in July and August 1980. In the company's history, this was only the second time when they travelled outside Europe for a tour, and clearly the experience of a different culture – the people, the music, and the landscape (that finds its way into the design of *Nelken* (1982)) – inspired and influenced the ensuing new piece(s). Perhaps this recognition, that the felt experiences a tour provides can widen perspectives and knowledge, and can enrich the vocabulary of expressions, led to the ensemble's new way of working: allowing new cultural encounters to animate and shape their new pieces.

These trips were a far cry from cultural colonisation; instead, they were led by the same quiet curiosity with which Bausch had always observed people around her; as she described: trying to 'submerge into the city, simply become part of the life'.[68] The ensemble approached their host cities with openness, humility and, of course, the awareness of the absurdity of the task. As Bausch noted at a press conference: 'I have worked in many cities of the world, but consider this now: how is it possible, for instance, to make a piece about Rome?'[69]

During the residency, as theorist Royd Climenhaga witnessed, the ensemble observed 'how people inhabit their lives'.[70] He noted that 'Bausch was interested in a variety of events, but was particularly drawn to situations where people move'.[71]

Back in Wuppertal, the new piece would grow out of the dancers' personal responses to their experiences at the host country, built from kinetic memories, feelings, impressions, motifs and music they had brought away. What made this process of interpretation truly global was that the 'filter' itself wasn't a homogenous entity but an international ensemble, with dancers coming from a variety of cultures and countries.

This new direction for Bausch and the ensemble perhaps contained elements of 'cultural anthropology';[72] however, the aim was never a description of what they thought of the country in question (as was often expected by the local critics). Instead, these pieces expressed how the ensemble and Bausch responded to the impulse they received from the people of the particular city during the residency: 'what these places mean for the people'[73] – the core of Bausch's lifelong observation of human nature.

Friendships, working relationships and further artistic exchanges were developed during the residency periods in various cities in the world, while the Wuppertal Tanztheater worked in Rome (*Viktor*, 1986), Palermo (*Palermo Palermo*, 1989), Madrid (*Tanzabend II*, 1991), Vienna (*Ein Trauerspiel*, 1994), Los Angeles, San Francisco, Austin, Texas (*Nur Du*, 1996), Hong Kong (*Der Festernputzer*, 1997), Lisbon (*Masurca Fogo*, 1998), Rome (*O Dido*, 1999), Budapest (*Wiesenland*, 2000), São Paulo (*Água*, 2001), Istanbul (*Nefés*, 2003), Saitama (*Ten Chi*, 2004), Seoul (*Rough Cut*, 2005), Kolkata (*Bamboo Blues*, 2007), and Santiago (*Wie das Moos auf dem Stein (Chile Stück)*, 2008, and *"...como el musguito en la piedra, ay si, si, si..."*, 2009).

By the millennium, Bausch had become a successful, internationally recognised artist. Her work had been honoured with several international awards. She had revolutionised contemporary dance by 'widening the aesthetic frontiers of dance and expanding the possibilities of dance, to the use of text in dance theatre'[74] and developed a distinctive gestic language.

The change in Bausch's reputation can be illustrated by an anecdote, recalled by Robert Sturm (assistant to Bausch between 1990 and 2009, then co-artistic director of the Tanztheater Wuppertal between 2009 and 2013):

> After the premiere of *Kontakthof with ladies and gentlemen over 65* [in 2000 – K.T.], one of the dancers (he must have been over seventy) went to Bausch and said: 'I must admit I am one of those who in the past used to storm out from your performances, but now I'm happy to

work with you here. I've received so many fresh impulses that I'm sure I'll live a few years longer.'[75]

But the fate of successful artists, so powerfully depicted by Heiner Müller, has come to Bausch too. Her later pieces, by common consent, are mellower, more commercial, and have lost 'some of the vitality of that early creative period'.[76] Bausch's visual trademarks are recognisable, even predictable sometimes. They no longer surprise or shock the audience. As Climenhaga noted, they are 'one step from the immediacy of those early works, and the step back gives the audience a bit more room for comfort.'[77] Re-admitting more dance elements into the pieces, as gradually happened from the late 1990s, they are easier to consume.

Was the softness – the optimism and 'brighter perspective'[78] present in the later work of Bausch – an artistic slippage or an artistic choice? Could this be the forgiving smile of a wise and ageing artist, seeking to leave some love and hope behind in a tragically confused and chaotic world? Climenhaga thinks so:

> The tensions of placement in a hostile world become the satisfied but slightly rueful look back at the struggles of youth. And there is a comfort in the work, in having achieved a place from which to say that which before was not possible to be said. Bausch created the possibility to say it.[79]

The new departure in Bausch's last decade's work was the introduction of video and projection into the choreography and the use of digital technology. However, she did not become an innovator of new media dramaturgy. Her new pieces remained within the (by now) comfortable and familiar sphere of the work of the Tanztheater Wuppertal –

still visually stunning and full of memorable moments, yet perhaps lacking the impact of the older pieces.

One motivator in the mellowing of Bausch's work is undoubtedly the fact that the ensemble – from whom the energy and the raw material have always come – has changed considerably over the years, with only a few dancers remaining from Bausch's pioneering ensemble of the 1970s and 1980s. The new dancers in the company were seemingly chosen to replace those who left (sometimes it is striking how the appearance of a new dancer reminds us of an antecedent member of the ensemble), and were doubtlessly accomplished artists, but, with only a few exceptions, they lacked the strength of personality and boldness of Bausch's early dancers.

The ensemble's lifestyle changed too. Perhaps because of the widening age gap between Bausch and her dancers, they no longer shared their lives to the same extent as in the early days. A few important friendships remained and deepened (such as with her long-time collaborators, Pabst and Mercy), but Bausch (although she did not take a break from working with the Tanztheater Wuppertal) became slightly detached from the ensemble. There was commitment and warmth towards her dancers, but the animated and close-knit relationships of the first decades were truly behind her.

A beautiful example of this former loving playfulness and teasing between Bausch and her ensemble in the 1980s can be seen in the film, *AHNEN, Ahnen,*[80] in which the dancers dress Bausch up in a grotesque, crocheted mask. It is like a sweet revenge from her dancers, as if saying: you ask us to do things that sometimes feel silly, now it's your turn to do so! As an answer to the provocation, Bausch wears the mask throughout the rehearsals.

Thirty years later the relationship has clearly become more hierarchical: Bausch is now the Master (or Mother), loved and respected but somewhat lonely. The generational difference between Bausch and the majority of her dancers reflects too in the working process.

Hüseyin Karabey's film, documenting the ensemble's 2003 residency in Turkey,[81] illustrates this plainly. In the rehearsal studio in Istanbul, Bausch sits alone behind her table, poker-faced, while the dancers one by one step to the middle of the studio to present her the movements they have developed. Most of the movements are clichéd, like caricatures of the Bausch vocabulary; they lack spirit, boldness, and the pain of truthfulness or the edge of experimentation. After each presentation Bausch nods, gives a polite but slightly tired smile and jots something down in her notebook, before quickly closing the folder. Her face rarely lights up in response to a new or exciting movement.

Yet she is searching patiently to find gestures from which, step by step, with precision she can build up a piece that resembles the song she keeps hearing inside, perhaps more optimistic than the old ones, nevertheless still distinctively hers...

* * *

'We have all come out from Gogol's *Overcoat*' – this saying (attributed to Fyodor Dostoevsky) suggested that the nineteenth century Russian novelists owe gratitude to Nikolai Gogol for laying a new ground for the genre. One can paraphrase that, and claim that the twenty-first century performance came out of Bausch's *Kontakthof.*

Bausch created many landmark pieces, such as *Le Sacre du printemps, Blaubart, Café Müller, Kontakthof, Nelken etc.* – works that even today, almost two generations after their premiere, continue profoundly to move and stir audiences with their honesty and beauty; performances that show human vulnerability, our desire for connection, and the various power games that we enact in our relationships. Furthermore, the working method Bausch developed became the foundation for collaborative theatre-making and creating contemporary dance. Bausch's method of asking 'mobilising questions' from her dancer-collaborators was developed in the rehearsal room together with the company and was groundbreaking in the dance context. Dance critic O'Mahony records the process:

> 'Pina asks questions,' says Jo Ann Endicott (…). 'Sometimes it's just a word or a sentence. Each of the dancers has time to think, then gets up and shows Pina his or her answer, either danced, spoken, alone, with partner, with props with everyone, whatever. Pina looks at it all, takes notes, thinks about it.' Famously, Bausch refuses to discuss the work explicitly and in rehearsals never reveals its underlying themes or possible future direction: 'Even the dancers have no idea,' Endicott claims. 'It's like a real big secret existing inside her – waiting, simmering, exploding.'[82]

Today we take it for granted, and fail to realise how brave Bausch was when choosing this way of working, when there was 'no tradition and no routine to fall back on'.[83]

In order to set out on this new path, it was necessary for Bausch to relinquish the role that was expected from her as a choreographer or director: claiming the knowledge of the end product at the beginning of the process.

> Then, at the beginning – I did in fact have a large group and in the rehearsals I was afraid to say, 'I don't know,' or, 'Let me see.' I wanted to say, 'OK, we'll do this and this.' I planned everything very meticulously but soon realized that (…) I was also interested by completely different things that had nothing to do with my plans. (…) I had to decide: do I follow a plan or do I get involved with something which I don't know where it will take me. In *Fritz*, my first piece, I was still following a plan. Then I gave up planning. Since that time, I have been getting involved in things without knowing where they will lead.[84]

Once this decision was made, Bausch became a facilitator of a process, guiding her ensemble through a journey to develop the new piece. It was a constraint that led her to a new approach for working in the rehearsal room:

> New was also the way of working with 'questions'. Even in *Bluebeard* I had started to pose questions for some roles. Later in the Macbeth piece, *He Takes Her by the Hand and Leads Her into the Castle, the Others Follow*, in Bochum I then developed this way of working further. There were four dancers, four actors, one singer…and a confectioner. Here of course I couldn't come up with a movement phrase but had to start somewhere else. So I asked them the questions which I had asked myself. That way, a way of working originated from a necessity. The 'questions' are there for approaching a topic quite carefully. It's a very open way of working but again a very

precise one. It leads me to many things, which alone, I wouldn't have thought about.[85]

These questions sought to capture feelings, memories, experiences related to the subject of the new piece. The questions to her dancers served as tools for Bausch to clarify the topic gradually and examine it from many sides. They also served as a device to create material when translating the responses about these feelings into a kinetic experience, a gesture, that could then be further developed into a phrase of movements.

'You always start with questions. Each person reflects, then answers. And then I work out the movements,'[86] was how Bausch summed up the method. It was never a direct journey, though, but rather a meandering through an unknown landscape. Bausch notes:

> It's like when you go into a particular subject and you start by collecting lots of little pieces. By doing this and also because of things that occur, other areas open up. You ask new questions. And you end up with a kind of collection of material which is linked, in a wider sense, with a particular subject, which may have a lot of ramifications. Then you start to work with this material, with all the little bits by putting them together; trying out a little thing here and linking it with something else.[87]

This collaborative way of working demands a different relationship between choreographer and dancers. As Salomon Bausch explains: this was 'a working process involving concentration and tension – emotional and physical – as well as trust and patience; an atmosphere (…) that can appear almost casual to outsiders'.[88]

Pina Bausch's documentary, which follows the creation of *Ahnen*[89] reveals the relentlessness of the work. It was a very draining task, hour after hour, to focus on an inner search with such a demanding honesty. It took a long time, sometimes it was painful, other times it was boring, and took its toll on the dancers, who grew emotionally and physically exhausted.

Bausch watched everyone's contribution, going through a huge amount of raw material, and taking notes. But it was only a small percentage of the dancers' responses that she found useful for the new piece. So the quest had to continue... growing the piece bit by bit 'from the inside out'.[90]

This new way of working was unpredictable and obviously took a long time. From the collaborators it required trust, patience and the ability to live with uncertainty. Yet this process had to be fitted within the mechanism of an en-suite theatre system, with premieres announced and tickets sold in advance, tours pre-booked, the appropriate containers organized to transport the set (ten tons of earth in the case of *Auf dem Gebirge hat man ein Geschrei Gehört* (1984)), and the set and costumes produced in time. It was a very vulnerable position for the choreographer, as designer Peter Pabst recalls:

> When she starts the rehearsals, there is nothing yet, no piece, no theme, no title – at least nothing that can be described. Of course these all exist, and she knows, feels the possible ways of approaches, but this is a precognition. At the beginning of our working relationship I wanted to know whether Pina had an idea, what the new piece would be about but, routinely, she always gave me this answer: 'There is still something above it, I listen inside myself, but it can't come out yet.'

I stopped quizzing her, because I understood that this is not a question that can be answered.[91]

Pabst developed the approach for his work as a designer when working with Peter Zadek at the Schauspielhaus Bochum:

> There I learnt that I shouldn't argue with the director about what something should be like, nor with the actors what it could be like. My job is to follow what's happening at the rehearsals, watch the actors and see in what direction they are setting off, and work out how I can help them in this by bringing a costume or a prop on the stage. Or helping them paradoxically by interfering: how I can disrupt them in what they are doing.[92]

He worked in a similar way with Bausch: following the work with the dancers, waiting patiently until Bausch was ready to talk about images. Then Pabst created several models for the set, discussed them with the choreographer, developing and refining their ideas, until Bausch decided which model she intended to use for the set.

Pabst recalls that this decision was usually made very late: between two to five weeks before the premiere.[93] From then on Bausch was working on the choreography with that spatial image in mind, while Pabst had the daunting task of getting that set realised in an incredibly short period of time.

* * *

However loose and intuitive this working process seems, it did follow a clear pattern. The first stage of the work can be called 'research and gathering of material'. This was the long time spent with questions and responses and their documentation. Dramaturg Raimund Hoghe notes of this phase of the work:

> Pina Bausch asks questions. The first weeks of rehearsals are defined by questions, four or five during a rehearsal, over a hundred during the course of the work. Calmly and with great concentration, director, author and choreographer Pina Bausch follows her ensemble's search for answers, for memories and (re-)discovery of their own histories. She gives individuals courage to make a personal statement, to follow their own thoughts, feelings, associations. 'Just try it,' 'No need to think in a straight line.' Initially criteria such as wrong or right don't have any place here: 'we often make such lovely mistakes.' Without immediately evaluating them, Pina Bausch listens to the answers, the individual histories, notes them on a piece of a paper, carries on with her questions.[94]

The responses or exercises gained a label, a shorthand or a 'code' (such as: 'Nazareth's scarf' or 'poem turned' or 'Janusz's nose') that was documented. This stage of the work, working with the questions every day, could take six-seven weeks. At the end of this period Bausch went through her rehearsal notes, choosing from the dancers' responses the most promising material.

During the second stage the 'longlisted' responses were re-enacted with Bausch deciding which had the potential for further development. In this way the material was refined, and only a selection made it to the third stage to become the building blocks of the new piece.

As development work began on these selected ('shortlisted') movements or phrases, the movements and gestures that came from the questions and exercises at the earlier stage become more abstract, more precise and more expressive. Bausch was watchful of every nuance (the rhythm of the movement, the position of a foot, the tone of a muscle etc.) and commented and corrected them. At this stage the dancers counted during the movements or used non-obtrusive 'work music' which only helped them fine-tune the rhythm of the steps and gestures.

The 'performance music' was introduced only once the movement was well developed – as an added experimental element. Pieces of music were tried and taken away. The same sequence was repeated to different music to see how each contributed to the quality of the movement, how it transformed it or counterpointed it.

The third stage of the process was the arrangement of these building blocks by juxtaposing them, and seeing how they work in relation to each other, and searching for an adequate form for the piece. As Hoghe noted in his rehearsal diary: 'A form that leads away from the personal and the simply private to prevent mere self-representation and self-revelation.'[95] This wasn't an easy task, as one of the dancers noted: 'the principle of being real is wonderful, but it's hard to find the right form.[96]

Although the characters and the scenes were developed from the improvisations and personal experiences of the dancers, ultimately everything was related to Bausch and filtered through her when working out the movement phrases.[97] Klett describes the process:

> Pina has a pile of paper scraps with all the exercises written down. 'Chairs Fighting' reads one; 'Suicide with Laughter', 'Men's Step', 'Narrow Shoes', 'Shaky Knees'. Every night in the Spanish restaurant we rearrange the

scraps in a new order. 'Line them up,' Pina says, and we try to order them according to themes or movements, music or dancers. This game of solitaire never ends, and sometimes we come up with a meaningful frame. The individual sequences change with the context in which they are placed, Jo-Ann's 'Ow Aria, ('ow' in all pitches and moods) turns from funny to sad when it follows a tired waltz.

When I suggest solutions to this theatre puzzle, I do so according to traditional patterns of action. I try to show a couple in their different stages or a character in its development. Pina finds this boring ('Now the whole secret is out'). She wants a total impression, from which the audience can choose the events it wishes to follow. Therefore she doubles scenes, complicates their structure by interweaving them. Many scenes run parallel, commenting on and overlapping each other. Sometimes ten different actions occur at once, then again everything is concentrated on one single event.[98]

Bausch's very strong sense of form can be observed here. Using simple tools (repetition, contrast, changing the dynamics or the tone of the same movement etc.), she created striking effects. The almost obsessive repetition of small patterns, then gradually changing their dynamics and developing them, using the structures of canon and fugue, are dramaturgies that are used by the minimalist composers of Bausch's time: John Cage, Philip Glass, Michael Nyman. Bausch (with her incredible instinctive talent for form) translated these tools into the language of dance theatre, using small gestures or simple movements as the units for repetition. Klett explains the reasoning, 'Pina doesn't want a continuous story line; that is too smooth for her. She seeks a logic coming from intuition instead of intellect.'[99]

Finally, in the last phase of the working process, the aim with the work was to further pare down the piece, removing superfluous elements and fine-tune the precision of the movement with a 'penetrating detail'. [100] This work didn't end at the premiere; in fact it continued long after. Often even the title was found after the opening night, with the subtitle filling in the interim: 'a piece by Pina Bausch'.

* * *

A characteristic of Bausch's choreography is that she avoids big, theatrical gestures, pathos, sentimentality or self-pity. Instead, there is a tendency to pare things down to the essential minimum.

The focus is on those small, mundane actions, gestures we would not normally find interesting or important; movements we would rather hide or ignore – but which can reveal a lot about our personality. Bausch is interested in these details, the tell-tale events seemingly at the periphery. For instance, movements with which people quickly adjust their clothes in public, or gestures of nervousness, tenderness, greetings or farewell. 'In the life we live each day there are so many things and bits of information, seemingly infinitesimal but in reality fundamental',[101] noted Bausch. These small, 'unimportant' movements gain significance by focus or repetition in her choreographies.

This dramaturgy of describing something by showing its fringes can be detected in Bausch's documentary of the rehearsals of *Ahnen*. Although the film tells the story of how the piece was created and rehearsed, it is edited in a way to avoid being the 'Wuppertal Chorusline'. The storytelling leaves out what would normally be considered as the centre-point of the story (a choreographer instructing her ensemble and the dancers responding to those questions); instead, it focuses on the edges of the story and shows us only fragments. We hardly see Bausch in the film, and never fully hear any of her questions or exercises. Her voice can occasionally be heard, but only in fragments, bits of instructions that don't add up to a complete speech.

The camera shows people preparing for an exercise, changing into makeshift costumes, practising a movement, turning a big dance mirror on wheels, or pushing a piano across the rehearsal room. Even when eventually we see a dancer performing, the camera only shows her shadow dancing on the floor. The only features the camera lingers on are the faces of the waiting dancers – creating portraits while showing their natural emotions: boredom, surprise, disgust, thinking or smiling.

Bausch's approach of contemplation on the marginal and moving away from the 'major' or 'theatrical' by focusing on the everyday or real; discovering a landscape by meandering round its fjords and edges, and describing a phenomenon from the position of a flâneur – is similar to that of Walter Benjamin. He also seemed to find profound truth in 'the charmed circle of fragments'.[102] 'How a convivial evening has passed can be seen by someone remaining behind from the disposition of plates and cups, glasses and food, at a glance,'[103] wrote Benjamin in

One Way Street. This correspondence of ideas places Bausch's work within a certain tradition of philosophy.

Bausch and Benjamin share a similar aversion to the full exposure of the truth: 'Nothing is poorer than a truth expressed as it was thought',[104] wrote Benjamin. And they both acknowledge the presence of premonitions and intuitions in life and work. 'Omens, presentiments, signals pass day and night through our organism like wave impulses,'[105] wrote Benjamin. 'I am trying to find what I can't say in words', noted Bausch.[106]

Another parallel between Bausch and Benjamin is the way they both look at childhood as a period of profound, sensuous knowledge, and that in their work they both adopt the position of seeing through the eyes of a child, unashamed and curious. They also use similar tools: by picking up seemingly innocuous, trivial details to say something revealing about the adults' world. As Benjamin wrote:

> For children are particularly fond of haunting any site where things are being visibly worked upon. They are irresistibly drawn by the detritus generated by building, gardening, housework, tailoring, or carpentry. In waste products they recognize the face that the world of things turns directly and solely to them. In using these things they do not so much imitate the works of adults as bring together, in the artefact produced in play, materials of widely differing kinds in a new, intuitive relationship. Children thus produce their own small world of things within a greater one.[107]

Apart from the framing, the focus, the locus of looking, we can see straightforward references to childhood in Bausch's work. Examples include *1980…*, where the ensemble plays various childhood games, or the episode in *Nelken* with the women dancing under the table, or in several pieces (including *Nelken*) where the men wear female dresses that don't fit, are too big and hang on the wearer awkwardly, recalling memories of children dressing up in their mother's dresses.

> When I look back on my childhood, my youth, my period as a student and my time as a dancer and choreographer – then I see pictures. They are full of sounds, full of aroma. And of course full of people who have been and are part of my life. These picture memories from the past keep coming back and searching for a place. Much of what I experienced as a child takes place again much later on the stage.[108]

Watching Bausch's works one cannot erase from mind the images of her childhood, hiding under a table in her parents' restaurant and watching the strange encounter of grownups around her in the room…

* * *

Memories of childhood and personal history are key motifs in *Bandoneon* (1980), the second piece Bausch made after her partner's premature death. In the piece Bausch examines her core themes: what does loving somebody and being loved mean? And specifically: what is expressed through tango, 'what's the use of tango?' – without resorting to even one tango step in the choreography.

The piece starts in a public place, a café, a bar or a dance hall – familiar in other Bausch works (*Café Müller, Kontakthof*) –

with high wooden panels covering the walls, dark wooden chairs and small round tables scattered around and a piano backstage. On the wooden panel there are coat hangers for the dancers' coats and scarves; above the panel, on the walls giant black and white photographs of people, portraits of boxers are hung that mainly came from cafés in South America, but there is also one photo of Bausch's parents.

The dancers enter, apparently wearing their 'Sunday best' clothes: three piece suits with ties for the men, a dress or light blouse with a dark skirt with high heels for the women.

The music for the piece comes from Argentina, mainly tangos from old, crackling records, mostly the compositions of Carlos Gardel.

What is apparent in *Bandoneon* is the sexual aggression between men and women. It also captures the essence of that feeling of battle and love that is locked in the heart of tango. Journalist Marion Meyer describes:

> Sometimes the women sit frontways on the men's shoulders and move in time to the music, while at other times couples dance on their knees, or the men and women cradle each other on the floor, locked tightly together. The steps are frequently slowed down, as the scenes stretch out and become a test of patience. Bausch is examining the rituals of couples dancing together and looking for new forms of unity.[109]

During the performance the scene becomes more and more bare: the tables and chairs will be taken out, stage hands enter with ladders, and remove the pictures from the walls, even the dance floor is rolled up. Yet the dance cannot stop.

Even at the curtain call, Dominique Mercy, wearing an unfastened white ballet dress, carries on with his melancholic solo ballet sequence, falling over, standing up, and starting it all over again, like a sad clown stuck in a routine, unable to stop dancing.

Meyer sums up one of the many thoughts the piece conveys: 'What does dance mean and what does the audience expect of it? The choreographer illuminates dance with countless scenic ideas and a sense that the performers on stage have to produce something.'[110]

Bandoneon was well received by critics,[111] but more importantly, it gained Bausch the friendship of Tete (Pedro Alberto Rusconi), the 'king' of the milongas and the doyen of porteño and waltz, 'whose feet seemed to caress the dance floor',[112] when in 1994 the company brought *Bandoneon* back to Buenos Aires.

Bausch invited Tete to teach in Essen, and to work with the ensemble in Wuppertal when creating *Nur Du* (1996). He also appeared in Tanztheater's 25th anniversary performance in Paris in 1998, and danced tango to the song *Pavadita*.

The open letter that Tete wrote in 2006, addressing all the young dancers of tango, shows many similarities between his and Bausch's thinking about the essence of dance:

> We do not have to dress up tango under any circumstances because this so passionate music gives us life, energy, pleasure and then makes us feel better. (…) I always knew that music is the main foundation of tango. (…) I would not dare to say that there is no technique when you dance but I think that it would be much better if they taught people to dance more freely, like for ourselves…there's

more fun there. (…) Tango is not a business (…). Tango is a part of our life, a part of our grandparents, fathers, mothers, brothers, sisters and friends. It is our life. We should not be so greatly mistaken and ought to conquer it again since we are losing it because we do not respect it. Dear friends, female and male dancers, (…) you should dance more tango.[113]

* * *

What makes *Bandoneon* special is that it is one of the few works by Bausch where the creative process has been fully documented.[114] The window for this is a rehearsal diary written by the company's dramaturg, and the first dance dramaturg in the world, Raimund Hoghe.

Hoghe's writing documents that period in the life of the Tanztheater Wuppertal when Pina Bausch's work was still considered risky and audience responses were unpredictable: 'Those days their work wasn't followed to the same extent as later, therefore my writings are an important documentation of the period, and Pina's work.'[115]

As a chronicler, Hoghe's objectives are twofold. One is practical: as he is involved in the work, the writing is the dramaturg's own 'logbook' which follows the process, recording its milestones, and clarifying his own thoughts about the performance they are creating. At the same time Hoghe has a journalist's instinct to get nearer to an artist and her working process and to record its sometimes mundane realities without romanticising. In doing so, he bears witness to Bausch's quest for truth and the right form to express it with the help of her ensemble.

* * *

At the time of his first acquaintance with Pina Bausch, in the late 1970s, Raimund Hoghe was working as a journalist based in Düsseldorf. He was known for his reviews and portraits in *Die Zeit*, and was commissioned by *Theater heute* to write an article about Bausch and her work. During Hoghe's first research trip to spend some time with the Tanztheater Wuppertal, he developed a deep friendship with Bausch that would later form the basis of their working relationship.

Hoghe recalls what Pina Bausch told him during their first lengthy conversation at her flat:

> 'What I do is watch. Maybe that's it. I've always only watched people. I've only ever watched or tried to watch human behaviour, and talk about that. It's what I'm interested in. And I don't know anything more important than that.'[116]

It was their common interest in 'watching people' that brought them together: Hoghe, in his work at the time, was writing portraits of people, both well-known (hence this commission) and unknown, everyday people, in whose lives he recognised something that spoke about the human condition.

Hoghe's essays about *Kontakthof* and the creation of *Arien*[117] were followed by other writings about the ensemble, as well as programme notes for the Tanztheater Wuppertal. He spent more and more time in the rehearsal room and with the ensemble after the rehearsals, discussing life, work and art over dinner, until, eventually his soft-spoken presence in the company's life merited a recognition in the programme as 'dramaturg' of the Tanztheater Wuppertal's shows. Hence the role of the dance dramaturg was born in 1979.

* * *

It seems appropriate that the profession of the dance dramaturg has a strong link to Germany, since the forefather of theatre dramaturgs, G.E. Lessing, was German too. Perhaps the tradition of theatre dramaturgy in Germany played its part in allowing a name to be so easily found for Hoghe's role.

When Hoghe joined Bausch's creative endeavours in 1979, there were already many theatre dramaturgs working in Germany, so there was already an established role and working protocols to refer to. However, the role of the dramaturg was a new area in the field of dance. The space for such a role seemingly opened up with the new way of creating contemporary dance – a method that Bausch pioneered. This collaborative approach, employing improvisation, intuition and 'connected thinking',[118] has been embraced by various choreographers and dramaturgs ever since. Dramaturg and theorist Marianne Van Kerkhoven describes the process this way:

> We consciously choose material from various origins (texts, movements, film images, objects, ideas etc.); the 'human material' (actors/dancers) clearly prevails over the rest; the performers' personalities and not their technical capacities are the creation's foundation. The director or choreographer starts off with those materials: in the course of the rehearsal process he/she observes how the materials behave and develop; only at the end of this entire process do we gradually distinguish a concept,

a structure, a more or less clearly outlined form; this structure is by no means known at the start.[119]

Dramaturg and theorist Guy Cools points out the dramaturg's role in this process as one who 'stimulates the creative (...) intuition of the involved bodies and helps the choreographer to structure this intuition in its proper logic.'[120]

It would take another fifteen years for this new working process (in which the work in the rehearsal room is not about the interpretation of an already written play/choreography, but is a gradual generation process of a new piece) to be recognised and for its dramaturgy to be distinguished as 'new dramaturgy'. The term was coined by Van Kerkhoven:

> [It is a] quest for possible understanding, [where] the meaning, the intentions, the form and the substance of a play arise during the working process (...). In this case dramaturgy is no longer a means of bringing out the structure of the meaning of the world in a play, but (a quest for) a provisional or possible arrangement which the artist imposes on those elements he gathers from a reality that appears to him chaotic. In this kind of world picture, causality and linearity lose their value, storyline and psychologically explicable characters are put at risk, there is no longer a hierarchy amongst the artistic building blocks used...[121]

As for Bausch and Hoghe, they cared little at the time that with the naming of his role they were writing history and launching new dramaturgy and the career of the dance dramaturg. For them this collaboration was the meeting of concordant minds, brought together by their friendship and their 'similarity of tastes and interests'.[122]

* * *

Hoghe first met Bausch during a particularly difficult time in her life: her partner and the designer for the Tanztheater Wuppertal, Rolf Borzik, was seriously ill.

Borzik attended the Folkwang-Hochscule in Essen in 1967, to study graphics and design. There he met Bausch, who at that time was working at the Folkwang Ballet. The friendship grew into a relationship, both personal and professional. After Bausch's appointment in Wuppertal, Borzik became the designer of set, lighting and costumes for all her pieces. When Borzik died in 1980, Bausch lost her closest ally. She was also anxious that without Borzik's support she may not even be able to continue her work.[123]

Hoghe, as a good friend, recognised this insecurity, and supported Bausch and her determination to keep making work. By then he had become a regular presence in the rehearsal room, so it was natural that his role gradually increased to take on some of that dialogue-relationship Bausch used to have with Borzik. *1980 – Ein Stück von Pina Bausch* (1980) is the first performance for which on the programme Hoghe's name is found as the dramaturg of the production.

1980... and the following work, *Bandoneon* (1980), remained close to Bausch's heart,[124] because through them she managed to deal with her trauma; and by holding onto her work, to carry on with her personal and professional life.

Hoghe saw this support as his chief role as Bausch's dramaturg: 'I wanted to support her, so she could do what she wanted. This is how I understood my role as her dramaturg. It was a deep friendship.'[125] He brought many qualities to his role. His thoughts on life and art corresponded with Bausch's. They shared similar ideas on taste and form. He provided encouragement and emotional support (expressed through an often quiet but reassuring presence in the rehearsal room), and was supportive without being subservient, intelligent without being ostentatious. He had an artistic sensibility, but was somebody with his own individual personality and interests.

Hoghe notes: 'Pina didn't ask people to come to the rehearsals to give comments; she made the pieces she wanted to see. And I liked this very much about her.'[126] Hoghe knew Bausch's aversion to spelling things out, pinning down meanings, so in his work (be it programme notes or rehearsal diary) he also left open the possibility for different interpretations.

* * *

'What is the point of tango?'[127] – this is one of the main questions that Pina Bausch asks when developing the new performance that would later receive the title, *Bandoneon*.

The place is the Lichtburg, a disused cinema. The building is divided into two: in the front a McDonald's, a temple for fast food commodity, and in the back, where once the cinema's auditorium used to be, the Tanztheater's rehearsal room: 'a huge, empty space with a couple of dozen chairs, old armchairs and wooden tables, ripped sofas, high wardrobe mirrors, bright green plastic wall-covering, narrow, yellow cinema lights, a white screen'.[128] A stark contrast between what goes on in the front and in the back of the building: in the front one of the emblems of consumer capitalism; in the back a unique contemporary ensemble, creating 'slow-cooked' productions, relying on the personalities and individual experiences and memories of the dancers.

The piece is not yet known, it has no title. What is certain though is that it will be premiered in December. There are dancers and two actors in it, and Bausch takes her inspiration from the company's South American tour.

Hoghe, the dramaturg of the production, comes regularly, and records and documents the rehearsal process in his diary. The text is written with the inquisitive mind of a journalist, the skills of a writer, and with the sensibility of an artist. It is an intimate and personal document written by an insider who finds sympathy and warmth towards the ensemble. Hoghe often uses a form of shorthand, words that recollect the image of an exercise, or a feeling it evoked. He records the stages of the work, his own thoughts and associations, as well as Bausch's remarks, that – although referring to a particular point in the rehearsal – taken out of context can be imbued with even deeper meaning.

For instance, after practising various tricks with hats, Hoghe writes: '"The hat tricks," says Pina Bausch on one occasion, "should detain, like a goodbye."'[129]

And in that remark one catches a glimpse of Bausch's stage aesthetics (or dramaturgy): paring things down, keeping them simple, but also not laying everything bare, 'to gain insights yet keep secrets'.[130] 'Of course I can say more, but then I would no longer need to ask any questions,' [131] Hoghe quotes her.

The process of creating a new piece that as yet has no name and is inspired by the Argentinian tango begins with memories and exercises – and Bausch's 'trademark' questions. Although no one knows what the new piece will be like, Hoghe emphasises that the questions are not aimless or interchangeable: 'Even though it is still not possible to work out in what direction the piece is going, the questions are nevertheless looking for and circling around something specific – it just remains unspoken.'[132]

As Bausch's dramaturg, Hoghe watches and notes down the responses to those questions, images and movements that stick in his mind, as well as his own associations, feelings or just frustration and speechlessness when the dancers' replies are obvious, commonplace, redundant.[133]

Hoghe's writing reveals an intimate knowledge of the ensemble and their way of working. His notes also protect the dancers: he never shares the owner of a memory or a reply; the reader only learns that the response came from a male or female member of the ensemble.

The diary also shows what an attentive observer and expressive describer Hoghe is: depicting the dancers' movements and action succinctly, creating a powerful image in the reader's mind with only a few words. Yet, at the end of one of his entries he remarks on the impossibility of the task:

> The desire to talk about images, situations, stories of Pina Bausch is in direct contradiction to the feeling that you can't reach them with words, only diminish them, that you can convey only very narrowly the parallels of different realities manifested on the stage: the breadth of the space and its closed nature, for example, the hit songs from the Thirties and the feelings that are not so far away, the bright yellow, pink, turquoise, green, blue,

violet of the cocktail dresses, the flattened pomaded hair
of the men and the awkward relationships, the inept
and often hurtful efforts and attempts at tenderness.[134]

Hoghe follows the work with patience, recording the way it develops step by step, as if the ensemble is putting together a puzzle, except that there is no pre-existing image being recreated, only their embodied knowledge and felt experience to rely on about connections between people.

Two weeks into the rehearsals and key motifs are emerging: small 'moments of tenderness and aggression',[135] and memories of experiencing the same thing differently. Themes of self-protection and strength develop, that lead Hoghe to further discovery about Bausch's work: 'During rehearsals Pina Bausch probes things that one does in order to disguise one's vulnerability.'[136] Personal history and memories of childhood become a recurring motif in the work – which prompts an exercise that Hoghe suggests: to bring in childhood photos and make comments on them, loose associations on their own childhood and vulnerabilities. The results of this exercise, childhood photos of the ensemble members, with their accompanying notes (some confessional, others ironic) become the programme for the show. (It is also included in this volume.)

Hoghe knows Bausch as a confidant, connecting with her instinctively and understanding her artistic world profoundly. But he is discreet: although he shows Bausch at work in detail, he does not uncover her fully, nor is he sensationalist in his writing. The diary reads like the account of an intelligent collaborator in the ensemble and a sensitive friend. He is also wise: he knows that words can only partially express how the ensemble, with their gestures (movements, set, music etc.), have set about to capture the elusive nature of truth.

The diary records that the work is a combination of effort and serendipity. Hoghe tells of an incident during the dress rehearsal at the Opera house, where, frustrated by the overrunning rehearsal, the stage hands walked on the stage, dismantled the set and rolled up the dance floor. The ensemble carried on dancing in a space as it grew bigger and bleaker – and Bausch recognised that this was a feeling she was looking for. So by next evening's premiere she swapped the two acts of the piece and made the disassembling of the set by the stagehands a feature of the performance.

Finally a title is found for the piece (just in time for the premiere). However, the first public opening is not the final destination of the journey:

> The premiere of *Bandoneon*: not the end. The work is not finished. The piece develops further over the next few weeks. Scenes are swapped. Stories removed. Others added. Following a performance in February, two months after the premiere, Pina Bausch declared: 'We're still en route.'[137]

* * *

Hoghe is humble: he reveals little of his role as a dramaturg in the process and his contribution towards the work. His work is considered as if it goes without saying. Only when his work steps out of the ordinary, such as visiting a pet shop to find out about the behaviour of mice for the show, does Hoghe describe his work in detail – and this is then done with a gentle sense of humour.

However modest its writer, the diary reveals much about the chronicler and his artistic sensibility. One example is the way the motifs and themes that occur in the rehearsal room affect and captivate him, and lead him onto related subjects outside the rehearsal room, on his way home, or on the street. He connects these 'real world' experiences with the theme of the day, muses on them, and one can imagine that in his quiet way he releases them back into the rehearsal room or during a discussion after work. As he well knows, all these little moments and feelings are potent, and potentially important for the forming of the work.

The themes brew inside him, they make him watch the world around him through the filter of the given topic of the rehearsal. If he notices something, a nuance, a barely noticeable experience, such as the client's words at the newsagents, after the rehearsal, he records it. By linking the experience to the ensemble's work in digging deeper into their own past and painful memories, Hoghe gives these details a more profound meaning – exactly the way they create the piece with Bausch from snippets:

> It is not until we put together the childhood photos for the programme that I find mine again. Somewhere at the back of a cupboard, put away in plastic albums, chocolate boxes, tins: photos, letters, traces of one's own history. At the station kiosk a woman next to me asks: 'Do you have my story?' The saleswoman gives her a magazine, 'My Story.'[138]

Hoghe's role as a dramaturg is to be present. Observant but not intrusive. Supportive but not interfering. Focused but not taking himself too seriously. Intelligent. Lighthearted. Gentle. Witnessing.

Although Hoghe has a strong taste and sense of form, he does not use it demonstratively during the work. It is Bausch who asks the questions, who makes the decisions, or shapes the piece. Hoghe is in the room to support the choreographer in her choices, to be consulted if necessary, but mainly to allow the work to unfold organically, the patterns and connections to evolve gently, preferably without his marked interference. As dancer Meryl Tankard noted of Hoghe's work as a dramaturg:

> I first met Raimund in Wuppertal over thirty years ago when I was dancing with Pina Bausch. Quietly, intensely observing our rehearsals and performances, taking notes, taking photos. Raimund was always by Pina's side. Deeply concentrated on every move, every detail, occasionally whispering in Pina's ear. He was a comforting presence during that very vulnerable creation period.
>
> I always felt Raimund's support and encouragement. He inspired me and he gave me confidence. Raimund was always aware of any slight and subtle change in performance and I always appreciated hearing his comments and observations on the work.[139]

This type of dramaturgy that is palpable at the evolution of the role of dance dramaturg is the self-same *decentred dramaturgy* that a generation later would be recognised by dance dramaturg and theorist Guy Cools. As described by theorist Peter Eckersall:

> Cools argues that dramaturgy as a process of collaboration is both generative and invisible in the development of work. He argues that it is not the role of

the dramaturg to give some kind of structural reading of a creative process, nor to assist in the organisation of these elements into a unity. Rather, the dramaturg is *facilitating a process*. Cools is provocative because he refuses to make simple interventions that might give a new work more coherence, maintaining instead that the diversity of the process must be shown. To the extent that Cools' decentred approach governs the compositional plane of performance and is intrinsically dramaturgical, this is also a model of collaboration.[140]

This gentle, decentred dramaturgy is very different from the active role of the Brechtian production dramaturg – it is almost the inverse of that interfering activity. It is a meditative and mindful role, an intense and felt presence, being devoid of effort or striving for action. An empty state of mind: open, silent, fully aware and relaxed. The dance dramaturg's presence in the rehearsal room might be described as an 'alert state of silence'.[141] He is open and very sensitive to the work happening in the rehearsal room, but his presence is not intrusive. Yet, this observation causes a 'disturbance in the system being observed',[142] and the end product, the performance, benefits from this 'interaction with the system' by the dramaturg. Perhaps we can call this the 'Copenhagen interpretation' of new dramaturgy, borrowing the term from quantum physics.

The other advantage of having a dance dramaturg in the room is the opportunity for working in a dialogue-relationship, which collaboration can be best described by the words of philosopher Gilles Deleuze, 'We do not work together, we work between the two…'.[143]

Hoghe accompanied Bausch on this personal and professional journey for a decade, building a strong bond with her, and worked as a collaborator on eight new dance pieces and a film. A decade later, once he saw that their tastes and interests were diverging (or perhaps they were changing), he gradually loosened his relationship with the Tanztheater Wuppertal.

After leaving the Tanztheater Wuppertal, Hoghe (like other members of the ensemble: Meryl Tankard, Mark Sieczkarek etc.) forged his own career as a dancer and choreographer. The works he creates deal with other topics than Bausch's pieces: notions of the body, our ideas about beauty, and how history reflects in personal stories; and they are on a much smaller scale. His own voice as a dancer and choreographer is distinctive and his work is recognised. Yet one can observe traits in his work that may remind the viewer of that decade of intensive collaboration with Bausch (or confirms the similarity of their tastes and interests): the love of big empty spaces, the usage of a long line of dancers 'festooning' across the stage in the ensemble pieces, and some echoing motifs. Bausch and Hoghe also share a preoccupation with presenting reality on the stage.

What Hoghe leaves behind as a dance dramaturg, is not only his involvement in and contribution to some of Bausch's most prominent work (some people regard this decade as Bausch's classic period),[144] but also a wealth of documentation of the ensemble's work – an indispensable contribution to our knowledge of the theory and practice of twentieth century performance.

Hoghe's work is even more valuable when accompanied by the photographs of Ulli Weiss (1943–2015), who from 1976 until her death documented the Tanztheater Wuppertal's work. Her artful black and white images recording rehearsals and performances reveal her intimate and affectionate knowledge of the ensemble. The ensemble remembers her as their 'long-time colleague and an important companion', a friend of Pina Bausch: 'Ulli Weiss helped shape a visual identity for Tanztheater for nearly forty years, contributing to almost all publications of Tanztheater – festival catalogues, book publications and programmes.'[145]

* * *

In *The Routledge Companion to Dramaturgy*, dramaturg and theorist Magda Romanska wrote: 'If the twentieth century can be called the century of the auteur director, the twenty-first century will be the century of the dramaturg.'[146] I accept this bold prediction with one slight modification: perhaps the twenty-first century will be the century of *dramaturgy*. It is certainly true that what characterises contemporary theatre and new dramaturgy today is the attention given to dramaturgy and dramaturgical processes. When theatre-makers create work where the text no longer has primacy, there is a higher emphasis than ever on dramaturgy: the weaving together of the material that will constitute the texture of the performance.

'There are productions without a dramaturg, but there is no production without dramaturgy,'[147] noted dramaturg Hildegard De Vuyst. This dramaturgy is none the less than, to borrow Hoghe's words, 'to build a clear structure. It is how time, space and rhythm come together in a piece. The 'empty' space that connects two points. That charged space that holds the work together...'[148]As a consequence of this, no theatre-maker (director, choreographer, deviser etc.) can have the luxury of leaving his/her dramaturgical skills under-developed.

I hope *Bandoneon* will accompany them on their search for the unknown.

RESOURCES

Banes, Sally, Terpsichore in Sneakers in: Lepecki, André (ed.), *Dance* (Documents of Contemporary Art series), London/New York: Whitechapel Gallery – MIT Press, 2012, pp.43-51.

Bausch, Pina, "My pieces grow from the inside out." With Jochen Schmidt, *Pina Bausch – Wuppertal Dance Theater or the Art of Training a Goldfish: Excursions into Dance*, edited by Norbert Servos, Cologne: Ballett-Bühnen-Verlag, 1984.

Bausch, Pina, Press Conference Notes, 2 September 1999, Goethe Institut, Budapest, minutes by Edit Csilla Somos, Dance Archive, National Theatre History Museum and Institute, Budapest.

Bausch, Pina, 'What moves me'. A talk on the occasion of the Kyoto Prize award ceremony in 2007. *Pina Bausch Digital Archive* http://www.pinabausch.org/en/pina/what-moves-me (accessed: 19 November 2015).

Bausch, Pina (dir), *AHNEN ahnen. Rehearsal fragments*, (filmed in 1986/87), a documentary film, edited version, Paris: L'Arche, 2014.

Bausch, Salomon, Introduction in: Steckelings, KH. W, *Pina Bausch backstage*, Wuppertal: Nimbus, 2014.

Benjamin, Walter *One Way Street and Other Writings*, transl. by Edmund Jephcott and Kingsley Shorter, London: NLB, 1979.

Bentivoglio, Leonetta 'Une conversation avec Pina Bausch' in Delahaye, Guy (photography) with Raphael de Gubernatis and Leonetta Bentivoglio, *Pina Bausch*, Paris: Solin-Actes Sud, 1986.

Berman, Janice, 'Dancing on new ground', *New York Newsday*, 3 June 1984.

Bernheimer, Martin, 'Avant-Garde Chic in Brooklyn. Hippo joins Pina Bausch and Co', *Los Angeles Times*, 3 October 1985.

Bowen, Christopher, 'Every day a discovery'. Interview with Pina Bausch, in: Climenhaga, Royd, *The Pina Bausch Sourcebook. The Making of Tanztheater*, London: Routledge, 2013, pp.99-102.

Climenhaga, Royd, *Pina Bausch*, Abingdon: Routledge, 2009.

Connolly, Mary Kate (ed), *Throwing the Body into the Fight, A Portrait of Raimund Hoghe*, London: Live Art Development Agency & Intellect, 2013.

Cools, Guy, 'zero degrees: Genesis of an Encounter', programme notes, *zero degrees*, Sadler's Wells, 2005.

Corboud, Patricia, (dir), *Auf der Suche nach Tanz – das andere Theater der Pina Bausch / In search of dance – the different theatre of Pina Bausch*, a documentary, Cologne: TransTel, 1991.

Croce, Arlene, 'Bad Smells', *The New Yorker*, 16 July 1984, pp.81-4.

Deleuze, Gilles and Felix Guattari, *What is Philosophy?*, London/New York: Verso, 2011.

E. Krauss, Rosalind, Mechanical Ballets: Light, Motion, Theatre in: Lepecki, André (ed.), *Dance* (Documents of Contemporary Art series), London/New York: Whitechapel Gallery – MIT Press, 2012, pp.37-40.

Eckersall, Peter, Paul Monaghan and Melanie Beddie, Dramaturgy as Ecology. A Report from The Dramaturgies Project in: Trencsényi, Katalin and Bernadette Cochrane (eds), *New Dramaturgy. International Perspectives on Theory and Practice*, London: Bloomsbury Methuen Drama, 2014, pp.18-35.

Gribbin, John, *In Search of Schrödinger's Cat. Quantum Physics and reality*. London, Black Swan, 1998.

Haring-Smith, Tori, 'The Dramaturg as Androgyne. Thoughts on the Nature of Dramaturgical Collaboration' in: Jonas, Susan and Geoff Proehl, and Michael Lupu, (eds), *Dramaturgy in American Theater: A Source Book*, Orlando: Harcourt Brace & Company, 1997, pp.137-43.

Hoghe, Raimund, Into myself – a twig, a wall: an essay on Pina Bausch and her theatre in: Climenhaga, Royd (ed), *The Pina Bausch Sourcebook. The making of Tanztheater*, Abingdon: Routledge, 2013, pp.62-73.

Hoghe, Raimund, On the way to Pina Bausch's "Ahnen" in: Bausch, Pina, *AHNEN ahnen. Rehearsal Fragments*, Paris: L'Arche, 2014, pp.65-7.

Hoghe, Raimund and Ulli Weiss, Pina Bausch. *Histoires de théâtre dansé*, Paris: L'Arche, 1987.

Hoghe, Raimund and Ulli Weiss, *Bandoneon. Working with Pina Bausch*, (transl. Penny Black), London: Oberon Books, 2016.

Iyengar, B.K.S., *Yoga Vrksa. The Tree of Yoga* (ed. by Daniel Rivers-Moore), Oxford: Fine Line Books, 1988.

Karabey, Hüseyin (dir): *Pina Bausch'la bir Nefés [A breath with Pina Bausch]*, a documentary, 2005.

Kisselgoff, Anna, Dance: Bausch Troupe Makes New York Debut, *New York Times*, 13 June 1984.

Kisselgoff, Anna, 'Pina Bausch Dance: Key is Emotion', *New York Times*, 4 October 1985 http://www.nytimes.com/1985/10/04/arts/pina-bausch-dance-key-is-emotion.html?pagewanted=all (accessed: 26 February 2016).

Klett, Renate, In rehearsal with Pina Bausch, in: Climenhaga, Royd, *The Pina Bausch Sourcebook. The Making of Tanztheater*, London: Routledge, 2013, pp.74-80.

Králl, Csaba, 'Bausch, a kérdező koreográfus. Beszélgetés Robert Sturmmal a Wuppertali Táncszínház művészeti vezetőjével.' *Revizor Online*, 9 June 2011. http://www.revizoronline.com/article.php?id=3367 (accessed: 9 February 2016).

Lartham, Daniel, 'Dancing Pina Bausch', *The Drama Review / TDR*, 2010 Spring, pp.150-61.

Linsel, Anne and Rainer Hoffmann (dir), *Tanzträume (Dancing Dreams)*, a documentary, 2010.

Loney, Glenn, 'Creating an environment. Pina Bausch redefines dance with peat moss, autumn leaves, sod, tables and chairs', *Theatre Crafts*, October 1984.

Lorca, Federico García, *The Love of Don Perlimplín and Belisa in the Garden* in: *Lorca: Plays Two*. Translated and Introduced by Gwynne Edwards, London: Methuen Drama, 2000, pp.43-64. (The excerpt in the motto is quoted by Raimund Hoghe: Hoghe and Weiss, 2016, p.76)

Meyer, Marion, *Pina Bausch: Dance, dance, otherwise we are lost...*, (transl. Penny Black), London: Oberon Books, 2016.

Müller, Heiner, 19 Answers in: Huxley, Michael and Noel Witts (eds), *The Twentieth Century Performance Reader*, Abingdon: Routledge, 2002, pp. 314-19.

Nádas, Péter, Pina Bausch, a testek filozófusa in: Lakos, Anna and Nánay István (eds), *Bausch,* Budapest: Országos Színháztörténeti Múzeum és Intézet, 2000, pp.9-30.

O'Connor, Patrick, (Tanztheater Wuppertal review, no title), *The National Voice*, New York, 22 June 1984.

O'Mahony, John, 'Dancing in the Dark', *The Guardian*, 26 January 2002. http://www.theguardian.com/books/2002/jan/26/books.guardianreview4 (accessed 30 January 2016).

Obadia, Régis (dir), *Dominique Mercy danse / tanzt Pina Bausch,* a documentary, 2003.

63

Oddey, Alison, *Devising Theatre. A practical and theoretical handbook*, London: Routledge, 2000.

Orsós, László Jakab, 'Én magam vagyok a közönség. Budapesti ebéd Pina Bausch-sal.' *Népszabadság*, 22 March 1995.

Pabst, Peter, Megtanulhatsz bolondozni in: Lakos, Anna and Nánay István (eds), *Bausch*, Budapest: Országos Színháztörténeti Múzeum és Intézet, 2000, pp.63-76.

Partsch-Bergsohn, Isa, Dance Theatre from Rudolph Laban to Pina Bausch in: Climenhaga, Royd (ed), *The Pina Bausch Sourcebook. The making of Tanztheater*, Abingdon: Routledge, 2013, pp. 12-8.

Poletti, Silvia, 'Pina and I. Leonetta Bentivoglio tells Pina Bausch's story' An interview with Silvia Poletti (trans. Rosamaria Viola), *Word in Freedom*, 9 January 2016, http://en.wordsinfreedom.com/pina-and-i-leonetta-bentivoglio-tells-pina-bauschs-story (accessed: 29 February 2016).

Robertson, Allen, Close Encounters. Pina Bausch's radical Tanztheater is a world where art and life are inextricably interwoven, *Ballet News*, June 1984. pp.10-14.

Romanska, Magda (ed), *The Routledge Companion to Dramaturgy*, Abingdon: Routledge, 2014.

Rusconi, Pedro Alberto ('Tete'), 'Let us learn to dance tango', 9 January 2006, *Todo Tango*, http://www.todotango.com/english/creadores/trusconi.asp (accessed: 25 February 2016).

Schmidt, Jochen, *Pina Bausch. A félelmek alagútján át,* (transl. Borbála Nagy), Budapest: L'Harmattan, 2011.

Schmidt, Jochen and Pina Bausch, "My pieces grow from the inside out.", in: Servos, Norbert (ed), *Pina Bausch – Wuppertal Dance Theater or the Art of Training a Goldfish: Excursions into Dance*, Cologne: Ballett-Bühnen-Verlag, 1984, pp.234-9.

Servos, Norbert, 'Matthias Burkert', *Tanztheater Wuppertal*, n.d. http://www.pina-bausch.de/en/dancetheatre/music/burkert.php?text=lang

Servos, Norbert 'Pina Bausch, an Introduction to the DVD', *Orpheus und Eurydike* by Christoph W. Gluck, a dance opera by Pina Bausch, a film by Vincent Bataillon, recording at the Opéra National de Paris – Palais Garnier, 02/2008, pp.16-19.

Servos, Norbert, Beszélgetések Pina Bausch-sal, (transl. Lívia Fuchs), in: Fuchs, Lívia (ed): *Táncpoétikák. A reneszánsztól a posztmodernig*, Budapest: L'Harmattan, 2008, p.218.

Servos, Norbert, 'Obituary – on the Death of Ulli Weiss', *Pina Bausch Archives*, 2015, http://www.pinabausch.org/en/foundation/ulli-weiss (accessed: 30 March 2016).

Sikes, Richard, "A Commentary on the Place of Pina Bausch in Contemporary Dance: 'But is it dance …?'" *Dance Magazine,* June 1984, pp.50-3.

Tobias, Tobi, 'Mood Swings', *New York Magazine*, 25 June 1984, pp.58-9.

Trencsényi, Katalin, A Portrait of Raimund Hoghe, An interview by Katalin Trencsényi in: Hoghe, Raimund and Ulli Weiss, *Bandoneon. Working with Pina Bausch*, London: Oberon Books, 2016, pp. 202-50.

Van Kerkhoven, Marianne, 'On Dramaturgy', *Theaterschrift* 1994, 5-6, On dramaturgy, pp.9-35.

Van Kerkhoven, Marianne, The weight of time, in: Climenhaga, Royd, *The Pina Bausch Sourcebook. The Making of Tanztheater*, London: Routledge, 2013. pp.278-87.

Wiegand, Chris, 'Performing Pina Bausch's 1980 – in her dancers' words', *The Guardian*, 7 February 2014, http://www.theguardian.com/stage/2014/feb/07/pina-bausch-1980-dancers-sadlers-wells (accessed: 28 January 2016).

Wildenhahn, Klaus (dir), *Was tun Pina Bausch und ihre Tänzer in Wuppertal? /What do Pina Bausch and her dancers do in Wuppertal?*, a documentary, 1983.

Williams, Faynia, Working with Pina Bausch. A conversation with Tanztheater Wuppertal, in: Climenhaga, Royd, *The Pina Bausch Sourcebook. The Making of Tanztheater*, London: Routledge, 2013, pp.103-8.

Zinn, Randolyn, 'Somebody Nailed my Dress to the wall. A Glimpse into the Work of Pina Bausch.' *3 Quarks Daily*, 25 January 2010. http://www.3quarksdaily.com/3quarksdaily/2010/01/somebody-nailed-my-dress-to-the-wall--a-glimpse-into-the-work-of-pina-bausch-by-randolyn-zinn.html (accessed: 22 January 2016).

Endnotes

1   Müller, 2002, p.316.

2   Partsch-Bergsohn, 2013, p.16.

3   Annette Michelson, quoted by E. Krauss, 2012, p.38.

4   Ibid., pp.38-9.

5   E. Krauss, 2012, p.39.

6   Pina Bausch, quoted by Jochen Schmidt, 2011, p.24.

7   Bausch, 2007.

8   Ibid.

9   Ibid.

10   Pina Bausch quoted by Hoghe, 2013, p.72.

11   Banes, 2012, p.44.

12   Bausch, 2007.

13   Pina Bausch, quoted by Meyer, 2016, p.19.

14   O'Mahony, 2002.

15   Ibid.

16   Just the fact that in certain Bausch pieces (*Café Müller, 1980…, Bandoneon, Walzer*) some of the dancers (Nazareth Panadero, Jean Laurent Sasportes, etc.) are wearing their glasses on the stage, is astounding. It makes the dancers presence individual, real and slightly vulnerable.

17   Orsós, 1995.

18   Obadia, 2003.

19   Servos, n.d.

20   This wasn't a strict rule, though. For instance for the creation of *Bandoneon* the tango music was the starting point, as Raimund Hoghe remembers. (Hoghe email to author, 17 March 2016.)

21   Bausch, Pina, 2007.

22   Servos, n.d.

23   Bausch, 2007 (excerpt translated by Penny Black).

24   Bausch, 2007.

25   Bentivoglio, 1996, quoted by Servos, 2008, p.18.

26   Bausch, 2007.

27   Pabst, p.71.

28   *Komm, tanz mit mir* (1977).

29   Bausch, 2007.

30   Zinn, 2010.

31   It is like a circus act, which is mutually dangerous act for the dancers (some of whom are moving with their eyes closed) and the designer (Borzik) who, in this case, was part of the performance, moving the chairs frenetically out of the way of the dancers.

32   Williams, 2013, p.107.

33   Wiegand, 2014.

34   Bowen, 2013, p.102.

35   Pabst, 2000, p.73.

36   Bausch 2007.

37   O'Mahony, 2002.

38   Orsós, 1995.

39   Oddey, 2000, p.4.

40   Ibid.

41   Orsós, 1995.

42   Schmidt, 2011, p.13.

43   Ibid., p.33 (excerpt translated by author).

44   Bowen, 2013, p.101.

45   Wildenhahn, 1983.

46   Williams, 2013, p.104.

47   O'Mahony, 2002. Raimund Hoghe recalls that the incident with the bucket happened during one of the performances of *Bandoneon*. (Hoghe, email to author, 17 March 2016.)

48   Robertson, 1984.

49   Kisselgoff, 1984.

50   Ibid.

51   Berman, 1984.

52   Loney, 1984.

53   Giffin, 1984.

54   Tobias, 1984, p.58.

55   Ibid., p.58.

56   O'Connor, 1984.

57   Barnes, 1984.

58   Sikes, 1984, p.50.

59   Bernheimer, 1985.

60   Clive Barnes, in the *New York Times*, quoted by O'Mahony, 2002.

61   Croce, 1984.

62   O'Mahony, 2002.

63   Poletti, 2016.

64   Nádas, 2000, p.9.

65   Müller, p.278.

66   Climenhaga, 2009, p.26.

67   Raimund Hoghe also considers *Ahnen* (1987) to include in the list of the 'residency pieces'. Although it wasn't conceived or rehearsed abroad, 'the piece reflects a departure into the new territory of foreign worlds'. (Hoghe, 2014, p.65.)

68   Bausch 1999.

69   Ibid. Bausch, 1999, (excerpt translated by author).

70   Climenhaga, 2009, p.27.

71   Ibid., p.27.

72   Ibid., p.29.

73   Bausch, 1999, (excerpt translated by author).

74   Schmidt, 2011, p. 148 (excerpt translated by author).

75   Králl, 2011, (excerpt translated by author).

76   Climenhaga, 2009, p.30.

77   Ibid., p.30.

78   Lartham, 2010 Spring, p.152.

79   Raimund Hoghe quoted in Connolly, 2013, p.34.

80   Bausch, 2014.

81   Karabey, 2005.

82   O'Mahony, 2002.

83   Bausch, 2007.

84   Ibid.

85   Ibid.

86   Bentivoglio, 1986, quoted by Servos, 2008, p.17.

87   Pina Bausch in Corboud, 1991.

88   Bausch, 2014, p.7.

89   Ibid.

90   Schmidt and Bausch, 1984, pp.238-9.

91   Pabst, 2000, p.69 (excerpt translated by author).

92   Ibid., p.68 (excerpt translated by author).

93   Ibid., pp.70-1.

94   Hoghe and Weiss, 2016, pp.75-6.

95   Ibid., 2016, p. 95.

96   Wildenhahn, 1983.

97   The fact that the dancers created roles and characters rather than just 'giving themselves on the stage' can be observed in the documentary, *Tanzträume (Dancing Dreams)*, Linsel, and Hoffmann, 2010, where former dancers of the Tanztheater Wuppertal, Josephine Ann Endicott and Bénédicte Billiet, (who themselves danced in the original version of *Kontakthof* (1978)), in 2008 as rehearsal directors help recreate the production with fourteen year-olds. Bausch herself explains in the same film: 'We find many characters in there, not just ourselves all the time.'

98   Klett, 2013, p.78.

99   Ibid., p.75.

100   Ibid., p.75.

101   Bausch in Bentivoglio, 1986, quoted by Servos, 2008, p.18.

102   Benjamin, 'Standard Clock' in Benjamin, 1979, p.48.

103   Benjamin, 'Optician' in Benjamin, 1979, p.83.

104   Benjamin, 'Technical Aid' in Benjamin, 1979, p.95.

105   Benjamin, 'Madame Ariane – Second Courtyard on the Left' in Benjamin, 1979, p.98.

106   Kisselgoff, 1985.

107   Benjamin, 'Construction Site' in Benjamin, 1979, pp.52-3.

108   Bausch, 2007.

109   Meyer, 2016, p.78.

110   Ibid., p.78.

111   Schmidt, 2011, p.79.

112   Rusconi, 2006.

113   Ibid.

114   Apart from *Bandoneon*, Hoghe wrote about the creation of *Arien*, *Keuschheitslegende*, *Walzer*, *Two Cigarettes in the Dark*, *Viktor*, and *Ahnen*. See: Hoghe, and Weiss, 1987. The work on *Kontakthof* is documented in Klett, 2013.

115   Hoghe in Trencsényi, 2016, p.219.

116   Hoghe, 2014, p.65.

117   The English translation of Hoghe's essay, Into myself – a twig, a wall: an essay on Pina Bausch and her theatre can be found in: Climenhaga, 2013, pp.62-73.

118   Haring-Smith, 1997, p.138.

119   Van Kerkhoven, 'Le processus dramaturgique', *Nouvelles de danse,* N.31, 1997, pp.20-21, quoted by Cools, 2005, n.d.

120   Ibid.

121   Van Kerkhoven, 1994, pp.18-20.

122   Trencsényi, 2016, p. 206.

123   Pina Bausch quoted by Servos, 2008, p.218.

124   Servos, 2008, p.218.

125   Hoghe in Trencsényi, 2016, p.209.

126   Ibid., p.209.

127   Hoghe, and Weiss, 2016, p.81.

128   Ibid., p.75.

129   Ibid., p.75.

130   Ibid., p.76.

131   Ibid., p.77.

132   Ibid., p.76.

133   Ibid., p.79.

134   Ibid., p.79.

135   Ibid., p.79.

136   Ibid., p.80.

137   Ibid., p.111.

138   Ibid., p.103.

139   Meryl Tankard in Connolly, 2013, p.114.

140   Eckersall, Monaghan and Beddie, 2014, pp.23-4.

141   Iyengar, 1988, p.XII.

142   Gribbin, 1998, p.121.

143   Gilles Deleuze quoted by translators Hugh Tomlinson and Graham Burchell in Deleuze, and Guattari, 2011, p.x.

144   Meyer, 2016, p.73.

145   Servos, 2015.

146   Romanska, 2014, p.14.

147   Dance Dramaturgy Masterclass lead by Hildegard De Vuyst, organised by the Dramaturgs'Network and Company of Angels; London, Moving Arts Base, 28 May – 1 June 2012.

148   Hoghe in Trencsényi, 2016, p.229.

TRANSLATOR'S NOTE

I approached Raimund Hoghe's rehearsal diary of Pina Bausch's *Bandoneon* with some trepidation. Hoghe is a not only an internationally-renowned choreographer, but he started out as a journalist for *Die Zeit*, and has written several books. So it was never going to be an ordinary rehearsal diary.

Although the diary follows the rehearsal process from day one to the premiere, it is written in a poetic shorthand that reflects the rehearsal process itself: an interweaving of question and answer, of text and dance, of private and public, of inside the room and outside, of obscurity and clarity, and trust. The trust that Pina Bausch had in her chosen ensemble of international dancers, the trust they had in her and in the process, even when they didn't know where it was heading. There is a sense of entering a realm so far removed from the modern world, where everything is spelled out *ad infinitum*, to a place open to exploration and mystery, where ambiguity leads to precision leads to more ambiguity.

The ensemble is international, as are many of the references, which sometimes gives the English statements an other-worldly tone. However, when it comes to fairy-tales, the Brothers Grimm version always stands: in their *The Frog Prince* the Princess does not kiss the frog, but rather dramatically throws him against a wall; *Mother Hulda* is an early version of the lazy daughter versus hard-working stepdaughter trope.

So how to read the diary? Not as a *How To Do … Pina Bausch* but as a guide to discovery of, and trust in, the creative artistic process.

Penny Black, London, May 2016

BANDONEON

A Rehearsal Diary

by Raimund Hoghe

8 October 1980

Memories: childhood, school, outings to the cinema, old films on the Lichtburg screen: *Dr. med. Hiob Prätorius; How the West Was Won; Das Haus in Montevideo; Die Tote von Beverly Hills; 40 Pounds of Trouble; Send Me No Flowers.* The cinema had to close in the 1970s. Today the Lichtburg cinema building is divided in half: out front a McDonald's propagates Big Macs and Fish Macs, coffee, Coke, service on an assembly-line; the auditorium however has been turned into a rehearsal space for the Tanztheater Wuppertal – a huge, empty space with a couple of dozen chairs, old armchairs and wooden tables, ripped sofas, high wardrobe mirrors, bright green plastic wall-covering, narrow, yellow cinema lights, a white screen.

Exercises. Trying out tricks with hats, casually, playfully. At some point each of the nineteen dancers has an old hat in their hand and is practising. Men's hats roll along shoulders, are thrown high into the air, caught, dropped, taken up again, thrown again. They're meant to land on heads, turn in the air or be caught on the tips of toes. Over the next few weeks different hat tricks are tried out and presented again and again, individually and in groups, slow and fast, in different situations and contexts: sometimes during a dance, sometimes sitting in a row against the wall. During one of these rehearsals it occurs to me how lovely it can be if a hat is just held – without any trick. 'The hat tricks,' says Pina Bausch on one occasion, 'should detain, like a goodbye.'

13 October 1980

Pina Bausch asks questions. The first weeks of rehearsals are defined by questions, four or five during a rehearsal, over a hundred during the course of the work. Calmly and with great concentration, director, author and choreographer Pina Bausch follows her ensemble's search for answers, for memories and (re-)discovery of their own histories. She gives individuals courage to make a personal statement, to follow their own thoughts, feelings, associations. 'Just try it,' 'No need to think in a straight line.' Initially criteria such as wrong or right don't have any place here: 'we often make such lovely mistakes.' Without immediately evaluating them, Pina Bausch listens to the answers, the individual histories, notes them on a piece of a paper, carries on with her questions.

'Everyone can think of something, do something like *The Last Waltz.*' One of the women holds her shoes in her hand as she dances. Another sits watching the dancers and a man sitting on his own – by the time she asks him for a dance, the waltz is already over. Isabel Ribas Serra sings a waltz to herself quietly. And: 'Can you imagine being in a magical meadow?' Dominique Mercy stands there with his legs together, lifts his arms, moves them like wings, flies. Malou Airaudo leads the group across a border; their movements slow down as they cross it, people become quiet, huddle together, hold hands. 'He takes her by the hand and leads her into the castle, the others follow,' is the title Pina Bausch gave to her version of *Macbeth*. Coming back, everyone is noisy and hectic again, like before. The moments of tenderness and stillness are gone again, utopia.

In between the individual replies I jot notes in shorthand into a notebook: *to begin with, this search in an empty space, on unsure terrain, without aim, without direction.* But that's incorrect. The questions are not aimless, nor inter-changeable. Even though it is still not possible to work out in what direction the piece is going, the questions are nevertheless looking for and circling around something specific – it just remains unspoken. 'Do something that no longer exists. Be loving-angry. Moments of defeat. Habits. Something with fate. Gallows humour. Rituals of couples in love. Six beautiful things from your own country and six from another. Make someone else jealous. Ask someone something and know that he will lie – without showing him that. Titanic. Hopefully no one is looking into my eyes.'

Federico García Lorca wrote in one of his plays: 'If things are not carefully and very cautiously covered – they will never be discovered.' Pina Bausch's questions are also attempts to discover something and yet not betray anything, to gain insights yet keep secrets. To let it all hang out is not her thing. 'That's where people make a huge mistake, they discuss everything down to the very last detail – until it fits right into their template.' Thus even in rehearsals Pina Bausch refuses to give detailed verbal explanations. 'Of course I can say more, but then I would no longer need to ask any questions,' she states in one rehearsal, and 'I don't know what'll emerge when I ask questions, but I don't want anything pathetic, anything sentimental'.

17 October 1980

Kontakthof, a piece Pina Bausch created in 1978, is being re-rehearsed parallel to the new work in preparation for its return to the programme. Rolf Borzik has devised a space for the *Kontakthof* (literally 'contact or meeting hall'): large, bright, two doors, one window, a piano, a cinema screen hidden behind a curtain, two dozen stools lined up along the walls that have women in glittering cocktail dresses and men in dark suits sitting on them.

A woman stands up. Goes to the front of the stage. Presents herself from the front, from the back and from the side. Pulls in her stomach. Bares her teeth, holds out her hands, feet. Presents herself from the back. Returns to her chair. On the tape an Evergreen hit is playing: *Frühling und Sonnenschein.* Three women come forward. Present themselves. Go back. A man comes forward. Presents himself. The other men and women follow. The whole group show their foreheads, teeth, hands, fronts, backs, sides. One woman smiles: 'Good evening, I'm from Paris.' The group goes back slowly. One of the women turns around: 'I'm from Hamburg. I am married'. They all sit back down on the chairs.

The twenty men and women form a line. Stand next to each other, behind each other. To music from *The Third Man* the group comes forward, their faces emotionless, their bodies bending at the waist. The group stops at the front of the stage. A woman laughs. Shakes her head. Falls over. Someone hums *The Third Man.* The group walks back. Hums the song. Sits down again.

A man in a grey suit pulls a toy mouse out of his jacket pocket. Frightens a woman. With a scream she jumps onto the chairs and onto the small stage in front of the screen. Squealing, she runs out of the hall, which is now empty.

Belly-dancing music. Women cross the stage diagonally. They are wearing high-heel shoes and demonstrate how painful these are, how they hurt, how they can't walk. The man in the grey suit follows the woman at the end of the row. She spots him and screams. He continues walking, slowly. Relaxes his muscles. Leaves the space. A little later the two of them cross the stage again, hastily, one after the other.

A woman in a little black dress comes into the empty space. She goes over to the piano, pulls off her shoes and tugs at her dress. Hits some piano keys. With every note she sings 'Ow'.

A second woman in a little black dress enters and walks in a circle around the stage. She is barefoot and is walking as if she is wearing heels. Pulls and tugs where her dress, bra and pants are too tight, restrictive, hurting her. The other woman joins her. A man sings on an old gramophone: *Mein schönes Vis-à-vis, ich bin verliebt in Sie.*

A man enters the space. Sits on a chair. A woman goes up to him and sings *La Cucaracha*. The man stands up and walks around the space. The woman follows him. 'You are very beautiful. Oh, you are very strong, marvellous.' The man leaves the room. The woman joins the others in the circle. A man counts objects and notes them down in a book.

A couple come in. Stand opposite each other. The man caresses the woman. The two women in little black dresses watch and give a running commentary. A man shouts 'Anne' into the middle of the stage. A woman arrives and follows him out of the room. The man in the grey suit is still counting objects. 'One, two, three.'

A woman walks to the front of the stage holding a chair. She stands on it: 'I am standing at the edge of the piano and threatening to fall off. But before I do that, I scream, so that no one misses it.' She screams. Everyone comes into the space and sit down at their places. 'Then I crawl under the piano and look out, reproachfully and act as if I want to be on my own. But actually I'd like someone to come over.' She stands up and grabs hold of a thin scarf. 'Then I take my scarf and try to throttle myself in the hope that someone will come along before I'm dead.' Music: the dancers come forward with sweeping steps. A man and a woman talk about food. A man lies on the floor – I wasn't aware of the moment he fell, I missed it as I was busy trying to record what I could see, to describe everything objectively, but it has all blended long since with subjective experience and history. The desire to talk about images, situations, stories of Pina Bausch is in direct contradiction to the feeling that you can't reach them with words, only diminish them, that you can convey only very narrowly the parallels of different realities manifested on the stage: the breadth of the space and its closed nature, for example, the hit songs from the Thirties and the feelings that are not so far away, the bright yellow, pink, turquoise, green, blue, violet of the cocktail dresses, the flattened, pomaded hair of the men and the awkward relationships, the inept and often hurtful efforts and attempts at tenderness.

21 October 1980

Pinch someone's cheeks. Pull a plaster off someone's skin. Be lifted up. Scratch. Yawn. Shake out your hair. Trip someone up. Stretch. Be serenaded. A hand kiss. Remove shoes. Undo a waistband. Look through the keyhole. Hang onto someone. Argue. Make a carrier pigeon, let it fly and then rip it up. Stroke backs. Bite an arm. These moments of tenderness and aggression are all answers to Pina Bausch's questioning about small moments of pleasure; they also illustrate how it is possible to absorb something completely differently, to feel it differently, to live or experience it in another way entirely, something that keeps on coming up during rehearsals.

'How do you know that someone suits you?' 'Sometimes you can't explain it,' says someone from the group, now made up of dancers and two actors. In my notebook I write down my own sense of being speechless when faced with something simple, obvious, commonplace. I note down further replies: 'Actually he suits me because he doesn't suit me at all.' 'I'm not choosy.' 'We both hate being alone, love asparagus, but are allergic to it.' 'He should accept the fact that we can love each other and that I can maintain an independent life.' 'That it's possible for us to fight and make peace.' 'I don't know, really it shouldn't have worked, but it did.' 'I like him because he is a proper man.' And repeatedly the observation: 'He gives me the feeling that he needs me.' 'I like myself.' One man reads out an adulatory advertisement about a hero and then relates it to himself. Later on, he re-enacts a group photo and places himself in the foreground. One woman shows a man her childhood photos and praises herself as a *wunderkind*: he looks in the mirror and with a smile, runs his hands through his hair. Using his hands, another strokes his body contentedly. A woman walks up to the mirror and winks at herself. I like myself: also games around one's own vanity and part of an attempt to admit something to oneself – even those things that are usually kept hidden. Out on the street I notice the violence in the faces of passers-by, visible signs of the effort required to control oneself, to keep up the façade, to show no weakness. During rehearsals Pina Bausch probes things that one does in order to disguise one's vulnerability.

27 October 1980

Childhood. Like love and tenderness, longing, fear, sorrow and the desire to be loved, a theme continually returned to in Pina Bausch's work. 'What have you seen in babies and children and regret that you have forgotten,' is what she wants to find out during this rehearsal, and she thinks of things 'where you think it is a great pity they no longer exist, regret they are no longer there.' 'Yelling and crying if you're not happy with something, quietly looking into the camera, playing with nothing,' is what one of the dancers remembers as something that has got lost. One of the female dancers asks: 'Have we really forgotten or do we simply think that we can no longer do it?' Pina Bausch does not come up with a reply straightaway. Later on she says, 'For me it's not about seeing that you can't do it anymore.' She's less interested in inability as in the possibility of being a child again, of behaving and expressing oneself as directly as children do, of being immediate, overt. 'My name is Jean and I'd like to play with you.' 'Carry me, I'm tired.' 'Why aren't you talking to me?' 'Playing with something for hours.' 'Using furniture as a castle,' 'Believing that a magician can do magic.' 'Always asking "Why?" – constantly questioning the environment and exploring oneself, experiencing and discovering oneself.'

Do something that you have no right to do. Gestures one makes when telling a lie. Lovely, lovelier, the loveliest. Something with two meanings. When one wants to say something beautiful or important, but can't. Moving someone so that they stay – 'Aw, please, do stay.' What do you do after you've held your breath for a long time? Make something very small into something very big. Erotic fruit and food. Which animals do you find erotic and why? Questions, themes and keywords from the previous rehearsals. At one point Pina Bausch asks the group to say something wonderful about men – 'There are so many wet rags, there's enough people without backbone.'

Tango. In the dictionary it is defined as 'Tango (Span.), (m.), Argentinian folk dance in a slow ¾ rhythm, spread to Europe as a ballroom dance around 1912'. Described by a poet as *a sad thought that can be danced*. In Europe distorted, flattened, sentimentalised. 'What is the point of tango?' asks Pina Bausch, and when she gets very little response, she states: 'But that is a lovely question.' Memories of reports from the group's South American tour come back to life: stories of old men and women dancing the tango with dignity and pride, the stance and style of the so-called ordinary people. – 'We might as well pack up and go home.' It is impossible for Pina Bausch to consider copying that and dancing the tango on stage. 'If that is what one wants, then one would have understood nothing of the tango.'

At some point Nazareth Panadero recounts a shy but stubborn advance in a tango café in Buenos Aires. 'There was a tall powerful woman at the piano and a short man with a bandoneon. Together they play a tango and stop. And the short man says to the woman: 'What am I doing? This woman seems always so relaxed and ...' And she says: 'Wait just a moment.' And he plays another song and puts so much feeling into it, and then he has another go at wooing her

– he is very tango. He speaks to the woman again: 'I don't know, couldn't we…?' And she says: 'Yes, but you don't have to go about it so fast.' And then she played piano again and the short man his bandoneon. He spoke to her after every song and the tall woman kept on repeating: 'Not so fast – you have to watch – wait.' And then they played another tango.

28 October 1980

The rehearsal work: continuing the search for experiences to which one no longer has a connection. An attempt to find that which is lost, for example, connection to nature, affinity, understanding. 'To speak with the wind or with the water as people used to do.' Addressing trees, grass, the wind, the sun – and failing. 'Something is strange here. Now it is simply an illustration and not a conversation. It has to have more to do with you, with your lives, your concerns. Perhaps you have to do something, maybe some work – so that something comes out of it that way', reckons Pina Bausch. 'I can imagine that when people used to speak to the elements it had something to do with the fact that they lived more lonely lives than nowadays – that they spoke to something as if they were conversational partners – because there was no one else to speak to.'

As I'm looking through my notes a friend interrupts and reads out a few paragraphs from a book. Amongst the quotes is the story of an encounter between a German ethnologist and a Japanese man who wanted to climb a mountain in Switzerland. When the scientist asked him if the mountains could speak, he replied: 'They speak and they don't speak'. I think he wanted to say to me that the mountains don't speak the way people speak, in Swiss dialect or in Japanese, but there is a way they make themselves understood. So if we don't define the word 'speak' too narrowly, then certainly the word 'speak' can be used.'

Even though in rehearsals the difficulties of understanding things accordingly were clearly apparent: what did not change was the desire to be open and experience the new. Pina Bausch carries on asking for 'a thing, something that one didn't know beforehand. Recounting something that one didn't know but recognised later – how was that, that moment one discovered something.' Mechthild Großmann remembers: 'Once I wanted to eat in a restaurant and there were tulips in a vase on the table – and out of pure nonsense I ripped off a leaf and ate it. It tasted amazingly good and since then I enjoy eating tulip leaves – the green ones.' Later on, when she eats a single tulip on stage, many audience members were convinced the flower was a fake. Yet again, the real thing is the most improbable.

4 November 1980

'Think about something with heart.' We are back in the familiar rehearsal situation: defining a task, pause, searching for answers. Someone stands up after five or ten minutes and walks to the middle of the space. Talks, plays, acts out his associations, experiences, stories. The others follow – for example with words, sentences, things personal and trivial, quotes from pop songs and familiar phrases with 'heart' at the centre. Greetings from the heart. Heart breaker. You can transplant a heart. To lose his heart. My heart was in my mouth. I lost my heart in Heidelberg. To break one's heart. A heart of stone. An artichoke heart. Dr Barnard. My heart belongs to daddy. Heart-shaped mouth. The heart can overflow. His heart is in the right place. To wear your heart on your sleeve. I place my heart at your feet. A fart is good for the heart. To have a heart for children. Hearts don't have windows. It is only with the heart that one can see correctly; what is essential is invisible to the eye.' In the end only three of these heart-associations remain in the performance: 'The heart is a pump.' The heart of a person cannot be replaced.' And the story from Janusz Subicz: 'When Chopin died in Paris, Polish people took his heart back to Poland. And his heart now resides in a cathedral in Warsaw.'

'How do you notice that time has passed so quickly?' A small moment: something we do every day. Destroy something. It's just so nice to be teased. Women's clichés. Do something that hurts yourself – but gently. Something with Maria or Maria Callas. Dance positions.

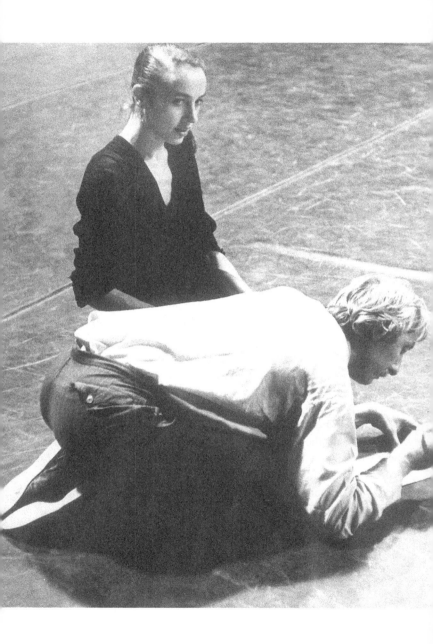

We're going to Italy. Do to someone else what I like physically. A change in yourself that is sad or horrible. And again something very simple: what do you do when you have a lot of free time?' Answers: Lie on the bed and stare at the ceiling. Read. Go for a walk. Go shopping in a leisurely way. Cook. Have a bath. Make a telephone call. I go out on the streets and see where that takes me. Visit friends. Listen to music. Play guitar or chess. What I'd normally do but I just take a lot of time doing it. Make love. Think. Flick through old newspapers. Learn a bit of German. Bake Polish cakes. Try to sing like Caruso. Be in the garden. Look at old letters and pictures.

Questions about what is – and what could be. 'If you – what would you wish for if you could start all over again? Where would you want to live and how – very very simple?' After several enquiries, Pina Bausch adds: 'Let's assume you come back to life, where would you want to live and how would you want to live, today. This has nothing to do with your biography and not even details like that, but in essence. A couple of things that might be nice. It is a wish but not a dream. It is as it is, as the world is today. Where could you maybe imagine yourselves?'

The answers come back hesitantly, doubtfully, from the members of the ensemble who were born across the globe; Australia, America, France, Italy, Poland, Morocco, Spain, England, Czechoslovakia as was, Switzerland and Germany. 'I don't know where but I'd like it to be a surprise.' 'In a warm country and I want to have brothers and sisters.' 'I don't want to start again at the beginning.' 'Travelling all over the place in a circus.' 'I want to be born where I was born again. The one difference being my father is alive.' 'I want to be a bird.' 'Somewhere in the mountains, a bit lonely and with a lot of woods.' 'There are the same problems everywhere, there is no difference.' 'Live in Italy at its heart and feel like a gypsy.' 'Near New York in a house with a large garden and animals.' 'In Asia, and then every few years somewhere else.' 'In London or New York, in a place where people develop a thick skin.'

After the rehearsals when we talk about the difficulties raised by the questioning of the past few weeks, Pina Bausch explains: 'I could ask simpler questions – but right now that would be wrong.' Simple questions are just not possible after the unnerving experiences, impressions and encounters of the South America tour: such as coming face-to-face with dwellings where you'd think life would be impossible; people in desolate environments; Indian villages in the desert – living that is a long way away from what we consider to be living. At some point during this evening Pina Bausch says; 'Loving is important'.

5 November 1980

Confessions. Injuries and vulnerability, strengths, weakness, contradictions and complexes, desires and fears, dreams and reality. After one rehearsal Pina Bausch says to her ensemble of dancers/actors/co-authors: 'I think it's great that there is a part of you in every piece, a part of your lives. There are other things that I think are great too, but this I find particularly lovely.' And in another conversation she said, 'Everyone should be able to be as he wants to be or how he has developed.' Pina Bausch creates working conditions in which that is possible. For people to admit to things: even their fears. 'If you sometimes have the feeling in certain situations that you're afraid, that you're not enough – what sort of fear is that? What is that all about? What is it that one is afraid of?'

Fear of being rejected, excluded, injured, no longer loved, is what I write down in my notebook. I gather intimate fears: 'Fear of doing something different to what I think. That I can't express what I want to express.' 'I always have the same dream before premieres that have to do with fear of failure.' 'Just saying something stupid. Being impotent. That my old friends seem ridiculous.' 'I am afraid that something embarrassing makes the rounds. That I'm fooling myself.' 'When I really like someone, I don't have the courage to tell him.' 'Fear of speaking to people to whom I'd really like to speak; complimenting someone because I am thinking, who the hell am I.' 'I'm afraid when someone says something lovely to me. Afraid of other women. Of nightmares.' 'Not being able to say what I mean because I am too nervous. Not being able to behave properly because I am inhibited. Fear of showing love.' 'Of being called a loser. Being unable to communicate fully. To say things in such a way that no one takes me seriously. That out of fear I say things that make me look weak.' 'Worrying people. Not having enough to do. Talking about myself because I'm afraid that others won't be interested.' 'Fear of saying what I'm thinking.' 'Fear of not being honest. Fear of not having any charm. Of not saying in words what someone else needs.' 'Fear of being unable to control my feelings. Fear of being misunderstood when I speak German.' 'Do you understand me? Do you understand?' asks a Yugoslavian immigrant on a train to Düsseldorf as he tells me about his life in Germany and finishes every sentence with 'Do you understand me?'

10 November 1980

Being certain. Assuring oneself. Being able to make oneself understood. Being understood. 'Uno, due, tre, quattro, cinque, sei, sette…' a woman counts on her fingers. Another helps a mouse to speak Italian: 'Buon giorno, signore e signora!' The groups says 'I love you' in all the languages they know. Another time they are dispersed about the space and count: in English, Spanish, German, French, Dutch, Polish, Russian, Czech, Italian, Swiss German. Sometime later they start counting again, to themselves and to their surroundings. Measuring the counts. 'Very slowly measure things about yourself. How wide is your mouth, your fingers. Very slowly. Take your time.' And another attempt, couples stand together. One of them measures themselves first then starts measuring their partner. 'And we can try it out for a bit of fun: you've danced, do that again with the woman measuring.' The man puts his arm around the woman, the woman measures forehead, mouth, nose, neck, arms, shoulders, eyes with a thread.

'Could you all quickly think of a fairy tale and a person? For example, Lutz is Tom Thumb. You say who you are and then perhaps one or two sentences, for example how it was between Tom Thumb

and his parents.' When asked what she meant, Pina Bausch replied: 'I think the only way I can explain it by giving an example. Sometimes it happens that someone is, or does, something that is in line with a fairy tale. You could say that you are a frog and when you're thrown against a wall you'll be a prince, or you're Mother Hulda and every day you shake the pillows. There is something real there – something happens and you are someone else.' 'I am Cinderella and the shoes fit.' 'Now the Emperor has a clockwork nightingale, but I will wait until he is dying and then I will sing for him.' 'I'm Little Red Riding Hood and I am hoping to meet the Wolf at Grandmother's.' 'I am the Princess and I've already thrown eleven frogs at the wall, but not one of them was a prince.' 'I'm Snow White and I've been asleep for 99 years. I'm hoping something will happen soon.' 'I'm Pinocchio and now I'm starting to live.' 'I'm the Wolf from Little Red Riding Hood and I've got to eat the Grandmother first.' 'Since I've been called Little Longnose, no one recognises me anymore.' 'I'm Dumbo and I'd like to fly.' On reading these answers later on, a suppressed memory of my appearance in a school play re-emerges: 'Thank goodness no one knows that my name is Rumpelstiltskin.'

Physical pain. How does one react? 'What sort of stance do you have then? Do you hold yourself there? Do you bite your lip? What do you do in that moment that you have a pain?' One person hits his head with his hand, hunkers down, sucks his thumb, touches the point where the pain is. After several dancers have shown their reactions, Pina Bausch interrupts and gets the group to imitate the different reactions to pain. First of all the women's reactions, then the men's, and finally they all do it together in a slow motion. 'And now do the same again, equally slowly, but smiling.' The men and women stand singly in the space. React as they did beforehand to the painful places on their body. But now the same movements and the stroking tell another story – they have an erotic and tender effect, are sensual and self-conscious. And as so frequently happens in Pina's work, what becomes visible is the ambiguity, the different readings possible for apparently unambiguous movements, stances, situations. As one continues to watch them, they become much clearer and yet at the same time more impenetrable.

12 November 1980

Pina Bausch's pieces: time and again pieces about attempts to feel something of oneself, to be sensible of something, to experience it – even in pain, even through effort. 'Something quite simple now: take up a position that requires effort, something that has to do with torment. It should be visible that remaining in this position requires exertion.' One position: Christian Trouillas takes up the bridge pose. Lies on his back, braces himself with his arms and legs and quickly pushes up his body. Keeps up the bridge and remains in this position until he is exhausted, then slowly sinks to the floor. Takes a break then tries it again. Tangos are coming out from the audio-tape, this is one of the first rehearsals in which music is being used. During rehearsals for previous works a great deal of music was played and there was frequently background music, however the tangos that have been brought back from South America are being used very carefully and protectively. The music speaks for itself with its own severity, clarity and concentration, simplicity and power. 'For me it is so held together – so that one feels strong – the energy is not simply thrown away,' admits Pina Bausch during one of these tangos in which there is no room for embellishment, disguise or masquerade.

'I'd like to pay and can you get me a taxi please.' 'I was taught that differently.' 'Nice blouse – is it new?' 'What? You're joking.' 'I already know that.' 'Sadly I have to go now but we can definitely speak about it tomorrow.' 'I prefer to walk.' 'I don't know, I have to think about it.' 'That doesn't suit me.' 'Do you not have any other topic?' And nodding, yawning, biting one's nails, stroking one's chin, hands over one's ears – examples of possibilities of protecting oneself, of hiding. Answers to the question: 'What do you do, how do people often behave so that others can't persuade or influence you – and so that you don't have to change your opinion?' In a later rehearsal Pina Bausch tries to connect the reactions with sentences about the sinking of the Titanic. 'All sit down together and then one person stands up and says something about the Titanic or another huge disaster – and the listeners do what they did during their 'not being influenced'. 'It's complete nonsense, I know that. I know already what that feels like in my gut, but I'd be cross with myself if I hadn't tried it out.'

'The Titanic was considered unsinkable. The musicians played on as the people were drowning.' 'Yeah, yeah.' 'I believe it was the maiden voyage.' 'I'm in a real hurry.' 'No one believed that it could sink. There weren't enough life rafts.' 'No, that's out of the question.' 'The passengers danced as the boat went down. Some of them had already gone to bed.' 'No thanks, I don't smoke anymore.' 'There were sharks in the sea.' 'That doesn't suit me.' 'Charles Laughton was fabulous.' After a pause, Pina suggested: 'React in the same way to Nazareth's poem.' Nazareth Panadero reads out a Heine poem from a piece of paper and goes looking for listeners. She walks up to individuals. *In the wonderful month of May, when all the buds were bursting.* 'Leave me alone.' *My love burst forth from my heart.* 'Nice blouse – is it new?' *In the wonderful month of May,* 'Why? Say Why?' *When all the birds were singing, I confessed to her.* 'Always the same old story.' *My yearning and my longing.* 'Let's talk about it in the morning.' I think about similar situations in other Tanztheater works: signs, calls, catastrophes that were not acknowledged or were suppressed. For example in *1980 Ein Stück von Pina Bausch* there were attempts made to get help during formal bowing and curtseying formations. Or in *Keuschheitslegende*, where Meryl Tankard played a woman who wants to draw attention to herself by calling 'Help' and 'Here' and at some point is simply left standing there alone.

14 November 1980

In the Adria Grill restaurant after a performance of *Arien:* a visitor tells of an actor who has committed suicide, I learn of the death of a friend. The person opposite me says that he was found in the morning in his flat, he'd been missed at rehearsals, the play was

Leonce und Lena – the author, Georg Büchner, called the play a comedy about love and death, boredom and longing. Later on I learn that the last thing they rehearsed was the scene between Leonce and Rosetta, before the journey to Italy. When I get home I look up the scene. Leonce says: 'Dance, Rosetta, dance, so that times passes in time with your dear feet!' And Rosetta replies: 'My feet prefer to get out of time'. The stage direction says: 'she dances and sings!'

18 November 1980

Images. I've noted them down and can no longer order them. Couples who bow and curtsey, then right themselves. People who get themselves ready for a particular occasion. Get ready in the middle of the space. Return to their previous position. Not doing what they want to do. Or: men and women stand opposite each other in dance positions. Talk of their fears of not being good enough. Couples dance. One woman waves her scarf like a flag. 'My scarf is kaput, my scarf is kaput.' And then cues: what is it we are waiting for? Ballerinas dying – they always die aesthetically. Tango positions. Very serious moments. What is the most important thing that you have, and the most loved? Embraces. Letting different things fall. Wishing to have something back. I'm hungry. Hiding something. A dream that becomes reality. Bluffing. What did you do when you saw the sea for the first time? Moments of being pure. Something important that happened to us. Is that beautiful, and then crying at the same time. What people say to a pretty child? Kissing everyone out of sheer joy. Practising in front of the window. An experience that you can't explain. Voilà. Inevitable. I think I'm growing wings. Carlos Gardel sits on a stone by the sea and sings. I'm just so afraid. I am not allowed to fall asleep.

24 November 1980

'I'd really like to try something. Dominique you try – Dominique dances and everyone thinks of something, not too much, but you do something to him because you think he's been dancing all day

– and you do something to make him feel better – realistic things.'
The group wipe the sweat from his brow, comb his hair, massage his
legs, give him something to eat and to drink, fan him, follow him
with considerate efforts. Dancing, the man being cared for tries to
break out of the circle of his besiegers, but is brought back in again.
Tries another way, creating space for movements. He flees from the
attempts at assistance, which look like attempts to capture someone.
At one point he stands there and causes embarrassment: his sex is
showing under the old black dress he is wearing.

'Could we get into couples again, I want to play around with
the tango. Could you do it on your knees?' In dance position, with
upright upper bodies, the dancers kneel on the floor. A tango is
played. The couples moved around the room on their knees – 'keep
going until you just can't anymore.' Knees start to hurt. The couples
go on dancing. Several try to hide the pain. Pina Bausch: 'You don't
have to hide it. It really is painful.'

'We tried this once before: one person did something and the
other maintained the dance position. So think about what you could
do, maybe a kiss, and the kiss is always maintained regardless. It
has nothing to do with the dance position. I just want to try it out
one time and see what is possible. See what it looks like if the kiss is
maintained no matter what one does.' Different possibilities are tried
out and then discarded. 'It has to be simpler,' is Pina's opinion. In
the actual performance Jan Minarik and Janusz Subicz say sentences
about the heart during the kiss dance. Heide Tegeder will make one
of the time announcements that interrupt the kiss. 'It is precisely
twenty-one hours, twenty-nine minutes and ten seconds.'

26 November 1980

The first phase of the rehearsal period is over. Pina Bausch makes
the first selection of stories, images, situations, sentences that were
created during the previous weeks: 'just a few things that I want to
look at over the next few days'. This is followed by a comprehensive

list of about 100 key words. Working with her, Pina once said 'is not easy, not for anyone'.

The next days and weeks are, if nothing else, defined by the search for a form. 'The form is certainly very important to me,' says Pina Bausch in one conversation, and if she is getting her ensemble to try something again and again, that has generally to do with looking for a form. A form that leads away from the personal and the simply private in order to prevent mere self-representation and self-revelation. 'It is like a role in a written play', she states as she changes the casting of one character. And 'it is not about someone vomiting out their feelings.'

27 November 1980

Remembering associations. Spontaneous repetitions. For example: 'Could you all have a go at saying what you're feeling – what does one feel, when one thinks one is in love?' Or: 'a sentence before you cry.' When I read through the answers again, they get mixed up. 'Little lamps get up.' 'It tickles.' 'I feel I'm completely without gravity.' 'Like springtime, when the energy surges out of the earth.' 'I need to speak to someone.' 'My body can no longer breathe.' 'My lips vibrate.' 'For a moment absolutely nothing happens.' 'Fantastic but scary.' 'Blowing up a balloon in your throat.' 'I take a deep breath.' 'I feel as if I have more energy.' 'Everything collects into something that hurts and has to get out.' 'I feel quite empty and my face feels really tense.' 'It's like a tickle.' 'For me – the eyes are tears.' 'It's like stage fright in your stomach, but you are enjoying it.'

'And let's do that sentence with the white make-up again.' For example: 'Very noble.' 'It has something to do with ethereal and soul.' 'Moonstruck.' 'Like my own ghost.' 'Black hair, dark red lips.' 'Transparent.' 'Someone who is ill and afraid.' 'A snowman.' 'Sorrow.' 'A man who is painted white would like to meet someone who is painted black.' Whilst I am noting down the associations I think of a fleeting encounter with a black couple on the street. As I walked past

I had the feeling that the woman had put black on her face in order to be the same as the man walking alongside her.

28 November 1980

Looking for associations. Trying out various possibilities: Can I see what happens when …', 'Another silly thing to try … no, that's not quite working.' 'Can I try something else?' 'Sit yourselves down on the floor and slide forwards – I just want to see what the shape looks like'. Connections are created. 'Could you all try to bring together the feeling of the tears and that thing with the heart?' 'What happens when Janusz and Nazareth dance and Nazareth reads the poem?' 'Could you try just touching different parts of the body and then going into the dance?' After the first caresses, which are not convincing, Pina Bausch says: 'You have to touch each other sensitively, not just hold an arm out.'

'Can you still remember the erotic animals? What happens when someone is sleeping and you say that to them. Do that to Meryl and Meryl can do her "I'm tired" and don't fall asleep.' A woman lies on the floor. Behind her the group stand in a semi-circle. The woman is trying to fall asleep. One or two leave the semi-circle. Bend over her. Talk about erotic animals: penguins, giraffes, swans, snakes, fish, cats, horses, crocodiles, and remind me of characters in a nightmare. After unsuccessfully attempting to sleep, the woman stands up. The group steps back.

Afterwards Pina Bausch suggests: 'Meryl, well, if she can't sleep – maybe she can do the whole thing against a table and not actually lie down.' As before she spreads her hair. Lays her head down. Breathes deeply. Puts on a blindfold. Changes position. 'I'm getting heavy. And heavier.' The same gestures, movements, sentences now tell a new story of loneliness and fear, dismay, vulnerability, tension and aggression towards herself.

29 November 1980

Smiling. Learning to smile. Being trained to smile. A ballet teacher: 'If you don't smile on stage, you're not a dancer'. Another corrected a pupil with a burning cigarette, held it under the raised leg and commented with a smile: 'You see, Madame, it can be done.' Meryl Tankard remembers a ballet teacher who pushed the dancers' heads under water, demanded a smile, and then stuck their heads back into the bucket 'to make us smile.' At some stage after a rehearsal someone had started to talk about their training, about teachers, breaking in, subjugation, being forced to smile. 'And if you can no longer breathe on stage, then you have to show your teeth and smile – simply breathe through your teeth.' Later on Jan Minarik tells about a folkloric ensemble who were forever smiling. 'They stood on stage for half an hour, came back to the dressing rooms and weren't able to stop smiling. They had genuine spasms in their cheeks.' In one text by Thomas Brasch it says: *The mask grows into the flesh and is called 'face'.*

'A lovely smile from everyone', Pina Bausch asks for in one rehearsal. 'But the eyes, I think, are very cold. It is not the eyes that are smiling.' The dancers form a line with frozen smiles on their faces. Cross their arms. Hold their hands firm. Talk smilingly about their fears of not being good enough. Walk backwards in a line slowly until they reach the wall. Wait. The line breaks up. They pick up a chair, practise again: feet together, swing one leg backwards and forwards. Lower the head, lift their arms – *pieds en première position. Batttements cloche attitude. Penché en avant. Port de bras en première, seconde, troisième position.*

A man and a woman (Dominique Mercy and Meryl Tankard) look at old photos. Laugh. Poke each other. 'Isn't it funny? You think it's funny?' Laugh more and more intensely. The woman jumps up, throws away her pictures. 'It's funny because you're stupid.' Runs to a woman standing to one side. 'Heide, tell me: Meryl, I admire you.' Yells and demands that her sentences are repeated: 'You are so interesting. And so intelligent. And your back is improving. I really enjoy being with you. I love to be with you.' Repeatedly corrects

97

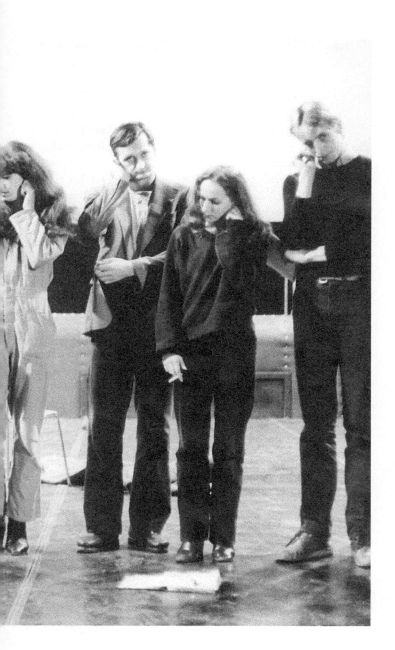

her echo. 'Louder. More clearly. I can't hear you.' Screams new sentences: 'You're changing every day. You're so strong. But you're stupid. You're really stupid. You're boring. You bore me. And why don't you learn German? And books. Read more books. Books.' She breaks off completely beside herself. Strokes her hair which is pulled back severely. Talks about a ballet teacher who used to throw shoes at her students, made them jump over chairs, hit their heads with her fingernails. 'You are stupid, Meryl. Really stupid.'

Janusz Subicz tells of the 'lovely end'. 'My ballet teacher always used to say: If you do something, Janusz, that is your business, how you do it – I really don't care. That is your problem. But when you do something, you always have to make a lovely end. The end is important, *très important* – lovely end – like this.' He opens up his arms, spreads them out and smiles.

1 December 1980

'I have a little mouse. It doesn't jump. Nor does it bite. You can stroke it,' Beatrice Libonati is holding a little toy mouse in her hands, sings a song for it. *Lache Bajazzo*. For the performance she is to have a live mouse. I ask about the behaviour of rodents in a pet shop. 'Usually they stay where you put them down.' A different pet shop owner is equally convinced: 'They are very lively. They'll jump away immediately.' Up until now I've been fearful around mice and not certain of their nature, I ask a third owner. 'As a rule they will start to scuttle around when you let them go free. But it is the same as with other animals: in a free environment they will stay where they are initially and try to orient themselves. Only after a certain amount of time will they move slowly and carefully.' The price for one specimen: 'Two Marks apiece – that's a giveaway, a real giveaway,' says the owner, talking about mice that are not given as presents: 'Many people use them as food for their snakes.' However there are no difficulties in supply, despite a solid turnover: 'We always have about two hundred in stock – in grey, brown and white.' They all agree that looking after them is easy. 'They just need some food, a bit of water and hay, so they can build a nest. Mice,' the owner went on, 'are the least demanding of all. They don't cause any problems. You just need a suitable cage for them.'

2 December 1980

A piano in the middle of the room. A woman climbs onto the piano and sings a love aria. Stops. 'I am so shivery. Who'll catch me? I had such bad dreams. I am cold.' Sings to the end of the song, climbs down from the piano and leaves the room. Another time she gets back up onto the piano, near her are several women on chairs and tables. 'It's just so nice to be teased.' 'I am a nervous wreck.' 'Absolutely everything is going wrong today.' 'I'm tired, I'm really tired.' 'People are coming.' Anne Martin sings a song, the notes to which she found at the fleamarket. *Such a pity, little lady, I would have loved you, loved you like no one else in the world.*

Isabel and Arthur – he kisses her. She says 'Relax.' In the evening she sings a love aria to a man who is walking beside her. A woman is sitting at a table and listening to a tango. As she is sitting there and just listening, I start to think that it can be enough when you just are – without all the stuff that one thinks one has to do to be loved.

4 December 1980

Picture. A woman runs through the space, spreads out her arms: 'Picture!' Runs to another spot, spreads her arms out and shouts again: 'Picture!' And again. And again. Then she stops. Vivienne Newport: 'In Hong Kong there are old peasant women on the Chinese border who allow people to photograph them in national costume for one dollar, even though they believe that you lose your soul if you let someone take a photo of you. When we met these peasant women, our tourist guide reckoned one could buy their souls for a dollar. One woman in particular stood out. She ran up to everyone, stood there and spread her arms and said repeatedly: 'Picture! Picture!' It was so obtrusive and so unbelievably sad that no one took a photo of her.'

I never cried. Meryl Tankard told us that when she had to go into hospital as a child and was given an injection, she never cried. 'The doctors, they used to invite adults and big men to come and watch me have injections, because I never cried. Never.' A man and a woman stand opposite each other and duel by slapping each other's faces. They show no emotion. Only their reddened cheeks leave any trace of the exchange of blows. Between taking notes I suddenly come up against a sentence that I can no longer place. The sentence is: *You can't cry twice.* Urs Kaufmann opens his arms wide, smiles and asks: 'Who will come into my arms?'

An entrance. A man and a woman in a long black evening dress come onto the stage. He presents her with a sweeping gesture of his arm as if awaiting applause. Both of them bow slowly. Their heads sink. She puts her arm across her breast like an opera diva. He says 'Gracias.' Someone is lying in a corner and crying. Jan Minarik teaches the group some football tricks. How to foul and simulate pain, knock your opposite number down and fall to the ground dramatically. The group follows his tips. Practise the tricks. Drop down. Take a dive. Are applauded.

5 December 1980

The first short blocks of scenes have come together like in a puzzle. Stories become cues, codes. For example: Nazareth's scarf. Nazareth Panadero comes into the empty space, takes a chair and places the scarf from around her neck onto a hook. Says a sentence from her own biography and jumps down from the stool. The others follow. They jam their scarves between the door and frame, into the piano, onto lights and walls, remember a sentence from their childhood. And jump; 'My mother gave me many things as presents – all stupid.' Jump. 'I was the first child in my family.' Jump. 'I was very blonde as a child.' Jump. 'Once I put my arms around everyone in the street wearing just my nightie.' Jump. 'As a child I screamed louder than my brother.' Jump. 'And after that my friend smashed my game.' Jump. And afterwards looking everywhere for new places for what one critic later described as the 'suicide game'. Parallel to the men and women jumping down from chairs, another woman talks of Father Christmas and of sinking of the Titanic. In one corner someone is doing ballet practise, undeterred. Someone else is trying to cheer up a woman and is singing: *Green, green, green is all my clothing.*

Standing against the wall like children: thumbs are sucked, sweets swapped, showing off. 'What is the sweetest thing and what the most important?' Shy glances to one side. Reciting of a Christmas poem: *Santa Claus is coming to town.* Parts of the body are revealed, carefully, fearfully, curiously. A skirt is lifted. Trousers opened. A bottom revealed, compared. Discovering one's own and other's bodies. As the group stands and presses themselves against the walls, I am reminded of the fear that children have of being found out during such explorations. Punishment, accusations, threats – of being put down in the cellar or no longer being loved, experiences that have been suppressed but that always reappear in dreams. Being shoved to one side like photos from childhood. It is not until we put together the childhood photos for the programme that I find mine again. Somewhere at the back of a cupboard, put away in plastic albums, chocolate boxes, tins: photos, letters, traces of one's own history. At the station kiosk a woman next to me asks: 'Do you have my story?' The saleswoman gives her a magazine, 'My Story.'

8 December 1980

'In Italy I had a chicken. It kept on going into other people's gardens and my mother had to kill it. That evening, when she had cooked it, she told me it was my chicken and if I didn't want to, I didn't have to eat it. But I wanted to eat everything. I wanted it all to myself.' Beatrice Libonati stands right at the back against the wall and shouts out the story from her childhood. In the actual performance she will only do it when she is all alone – and finally she goes and fetches a man into the space in order to tell him the story. And in other parts of the piece and not only this piece, both can be seen: people who seek out others and people who wait to be alone, people who push someone away and are pushed away. Like Nazareth Panadero with her Heine poem. She keeps on walking up to people with it, trying to get their attention and then drives them away. At one point she comes up to the footlights, pushes away a woman standing there. Looks at the audience full on. Has to wait some time for a tango to finish. When the music comes to an end she takes up her piece of paper: *In the wonderful month of May, When all the buds were bursting open, My love burst forth from my heart. In the wonderful month of May, When all the birds were singing, I confessed to her my yearning and my longing. In the wonderful month of May…* A few couples come over, push her away. The girl leaves. A new tango begins.

Tango. 'We'll just use the music – without anyone dancing a tango. During a tango the man only goes forwards or to the side, the woman backwards. Maybe the man can try to do the thing with the fire and to stroke the woman – or maybe something with a trick. I'd just like to see what it looks like. And do it over the music, very very slowly.' The men hold a lighter in their hand balled into a fist. They light it. Open the hand with a flame. Stroke the women with this hand. Pina Bausch: 'Do it again, but without the flame. I don't know, do the opening thing and the women have their arms raised.' The men open pockets, jackets, etuis, shoes, ties, collars, shirts. The women lift up their arms as if they've been shot.

9 December 1980

Sitting on one partner's knees, pressing them down into the floor. *'C'est bien pour toi.'* Play a few bars on the piano and flirt. A woman places two fingers on the shoulder of a man and lifts him. Practising falling. Exposing parts of the body and stroking them: exposing an arm, foot, hand, back of the neck, calf, stomach, shoulder, back, bottom and then carefully holding the partner's arm, foot, hand, back of the neck, calf, stomach, shoulder, back, bottom. Re-discovering the exposed parts of the body. Looking for a new place to stroke.

Cues. For example: 'poem turned.' Mechthild Großmann reads a poem out of a book. She walks in a circle reading. Stops. Loses her

balance. Looks for somewhere to hold onto. Sways. Grabs hold of a table, a chair. Holds on tight. Or 'Janusz' nose.' Janusz plugs up his nose and so can only breathe through his mouth. Cautiously he approaches a girl sitting next to him. Gasps for air. Offers her a sweet. Is unsure. And this helplessness is as funny as it is sad. At one point he comes on stage with his nose plugged and looks around the room embarrassed: 'Do I have to do something?'

A line is formed. Women sit next to each other on chairs and massage their faces, pat their cheeks, chin, forehead, temples. Stroke their eyebrows and touch their lips. Close their eyes. Behind them sit the men, distributed around the room. They stand up and walk around with their stomachs sucked in and their shoulders back. Take their jackets off and put them over their arms. Carry on walking. Put their jackets back on again and button them up. Janusz Subicz addresses them. With his plugged-up nose he asks them like a child would about Maria. The men say: 'Ave Maria. Hey Mary. *Ich bin Jungfrau.* I can't think of anything to say about Maria. She holds her head at such an angle. I've forgotten her face. Maria Robinson, she was the tallest girl in my class and the whole school was afraid of her. Mariacron. Marriage. *Je suis l'immaculé conception.* Maria Callas.' Finally a form has been found for the 'Maria' associations of the men following dozens of unsuccessful attempts over the past few weeks. During the evening rehearsal a form is also developed for the women. They are standing close together in a corner when Janusz Subicz asks them. They hold their noses and reply: 'Men in Germany are called Maria. Maria and Joseph. Ay ay Maria, Maria de Bahia. Jungfrau is also a mountain. The Maria in Santiago. Sky blue. Marijuana. My name is Maria too. I just met a girl named Maria. Maria Stuart. Maria Schell. My birthday, the eighth of September. '

12 December 1980

Applause. Being applauded. The women applaud the men, and the men the women. And then again. The women applaud the men who come out onto the stage one by one. Their reaction: 'Gestures that you make when you're really delighted but embarrassed.' And at the end the whole ritual is repeated. The women are applauded and they also have to react with gestures of embarrassment. At the fourth time the music starts. A woman takes a lemon and bites into the sour fruit, she enjoys every single bite. Lets the juice drip over her chin, her hands, her arms. Bites into the lemon again and sucks it out. The group moves away, applauding.

Sitting against the wall and watching. One couple stand up and walk into the centre. They dance. They bite each other's shoulders, neck, ears, as if they want to eat each other. The watchers pick up their chairs and sit themselves down diagonally across the stage. Remain uninvolved. Stand up again and sit down against the right-hand wall. A woman walks into the centre and lies down on the floor. She screams like a baby. The group look at her.

Leapfrogging. 'Could you do the leapfrogging very seriously? Sadly?' Leapfrogging: someone positions himself, drops his head, bends his back, supports his arms against his legs. Another takes a run up, jumps over him. The next one comes, jumps over both of them. And yet another. Jumps over them. *Ange bel ange* – a children's game. The women stand on chairs and the men run up to them. They clap hands and spread their arms wide: *'ange bel ange, saute dans mes bras ou le diable t'attrapera.'* (*Angel lovely angel, jump into my arms or the devil will catch you*). The women jump into the men's arms.

15 December 1980

A woman shouts: *'La mer – la mer!'* Jumps into the air like a child. Lifts her arms high and runs through the entire space until she's exhausted. *'La mer – la mer.'* She keeps on glancing to the side as if someone must come along with her. Carries on jumping in the air. Pulls the group along with her – *'la mer – la mer.'* This awakens memories of seeing and experiencing the sea for the first time, discovering water – something that appears in many of Pina Bausch's pieces. For example in her version of *Macbeth*, in which the dancers repeatedly let cleansing water flow across their faces and bodies; or in *Arien*, when Rolf Borzik filled the opera house stage knee deep with gleaming water; or *Keuschheitslegende,* when the sea froze and was painted onto the floor. In a school essay Anton Chekov found the description 'the sea was huge'.

Pina Bausch in a rehearsal: 'It will continue to be reduced – until only very small and simple things remain.' Reduction without diminishing. Also the language. Many of the words and sentences have become superfluous and been replaced by images. For example there are no words left in the associations to 'white make-up', instead the idea is implemented that the women have white make-up put on. During the rehearsals Pina Bausch reduces it even further – only one of the women is made up by the men of the ensemble – until she finds a simpler solution. Two make-up artists make up the dancer Malou Airaudo; they take white make-up and dab and stroke and rub it onto the body of the dancer who is alone in the space. Covered in white she then stands opposite a man, kneels down on the floor with him and takes up the dance position. Music: one of the tangos that make it seem so simple to talk about love.

17 December 1980

'A moment where something is one thing and something else, where two worlds collide.' The moment that Pina Bausch asked for – without great success – at the beginning of rehearsals becomes reality during the first dress rehearsal. On stage the stage lights go out. Workers come on and start clearing the stage for the evening performance. Tangos are still coming from the loudspeakers. The dancers and actors still performing on stage are uncertain and look towards the control desk where the director is sitting. Pina Bausch says: 'Carry on.' They stroke each other's backs, play leapfrog, give a kiss on a hand, bow very slowly, move away from each other. And in front of the footlights a woman remains lying down with her mouth open and appears to be asleep. Next to her the dismantling continues. The huge pictures of the boxing champion that make the people appear very small underneath them are removed from the walls and carried off the stage. Lights are taken down. Chairs, tables, coats, bags are all removed. The dance carpet is rolled up but the dancers continue to dance, to practise and to play on the wooden floor. The space becomes emptier and bigger, it changes, becomes simpler and more beautiful.

Evening rehearsal: back to Lichtburg. Work on scene processes, connections, chronology. The notes of the past few days have become ciphers: Maria. Cheek slapping. Entrance to Anne Marie's crying. Scratching Anne's back. Picture. I am not allowed to fall asleep. Malou/Beatrice dance. Hans Dieter Bravo. Jan rod. Make-up. Meryl I can't sleep. Hair-spreading. Couples come and find their place. Lift. Stroking the flame. Lift again. I'm falling I'm falling. Dancing on a lap. At some stage during the course of this evening Dominique Mercy puts on a tutu for the first time – the classical costume of a ballerina. It is old and yellowing and too small. It remains open at the back. When he turns around and walks away he has to grab hold of the tulle to cover his nakedness.

20 December 1980

Final dress rehearsal. The impromptu dismantling of the stage has become part of the performance and has 'derailed' the piece shortly before its premiere. Following the second dress rehearsal Pina Bausch considers swopping the two halves of the piece around. 'We could at least give it a go.' And she does so in the final dress rehearsal – the second half moves up and the previous first part is played after the interval in an empty space. I have the sense I am watching a different play: more encrypted and simpler, stranger and more familiar, clearer and yet deprived of rational classification. First reactions given in confidence: people are resisting the new, are against the loss of the old certainty.

Rehearsal feedback in the ballet hall. There is a lot of discussion about the open ending. At the end Dominique Mercy is to come back onto the stage in his tutu and dance, and practise. 'He should never

actually stop – just keep on going.' He remains as the last one in the empty space. Dancing, practising. Taking up classical positions. Slowly doing a *grand plié*, going over to another part of the stage. Lifting his arms, moving them like a bird. He looks around, as if he can't believe that he is not flying. Goes to a different point. Falls over. Stands up. Looks for another place. Carries on practising. A *grand plié*. Flying, falling, standing up, practising. When he appears on the stage for the first time in his tutu, he says: 'That's it.'

21 December 1980

Numerous suggestions for titles – Tango. Titanic. The mouse. The sea. *La mer. Corazón*. Who comes into my arms. Picture. In the wonderful month of May – are discussed and discarded on the spot. It is not until the evening of the premiere that the title of the piece is determined: *Bandoneon*. Later on I read a definition in the dictionary: Bandoneon, named after its inventor Hermann Band, a four-cornered instrument developed out of the many-cornered concertina. A bellows-driven instrument. Two notes on push and pull (bisonoric).

The premiere of *Bandoneon*: not the end. The work is not finished. The piece develops further over the next few weeks. Scenes are swapped. Stories removed. Others added. Following a performance in February, two months after the premiere, Pina Bausch declared: 'We're still en route.'

Bandoneon
A piece by Pina Bausch

Director and Choreographer: Pina Bausch
Set: Gralf-Edzard Habben
Costume: Marion Cito
Dramaturg: Raimund Hoghe
Assistants: Matthias Burkert, Hans Pop

Music: Latin-American tangos and waltzes

Premiere: 21 December 1980, Wuppertal Opera House

Cast of the premiere:

Malou Airaudo

Anne Marie Benati

Mechthild Großmann

Urs Kaufmann

Hans Dieter Knebel

Beatrice Libonati

Anne Martin

Dominique Mercy

Jan Minarik

Vivienne Newport

Nazareth Panadero

Isabel Ribas Serra

Arthur Rosenfeld

Jean-Laurent Sasportes

Janusz Subicz

Meryl Tankard

Heide Tegeder

Christian Trouillas

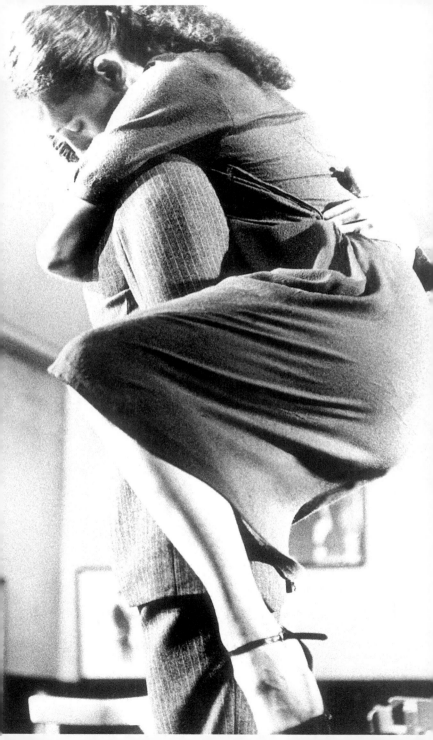

124

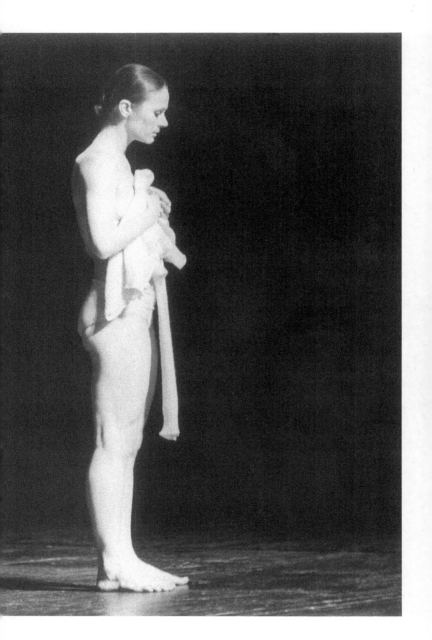

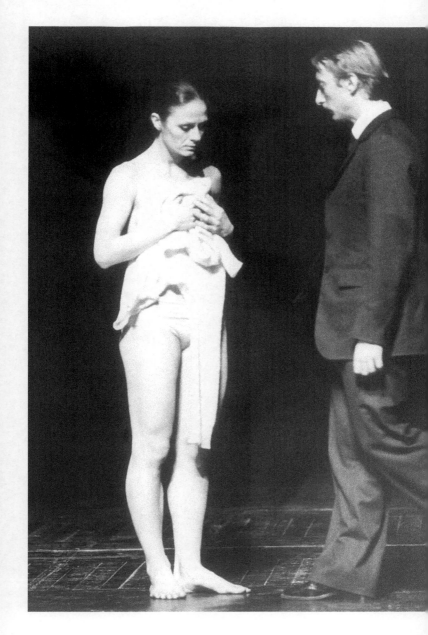

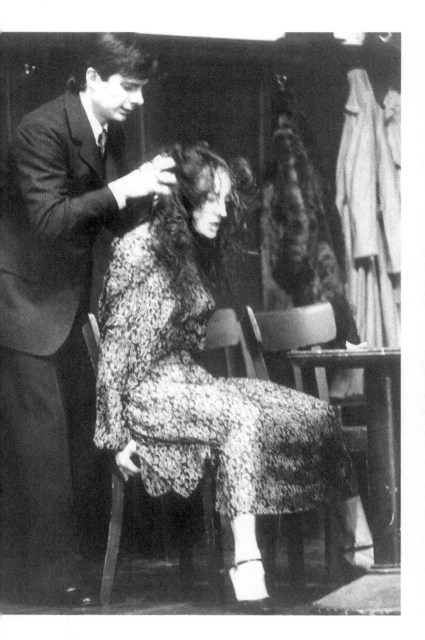

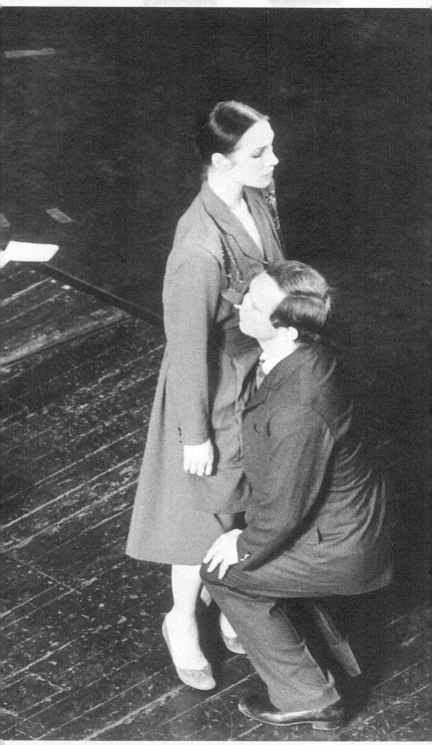

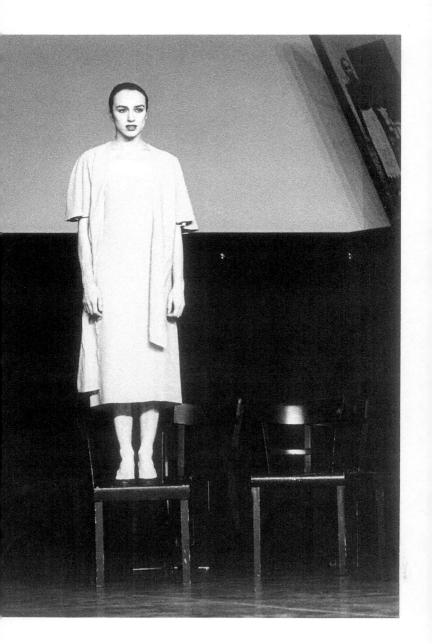

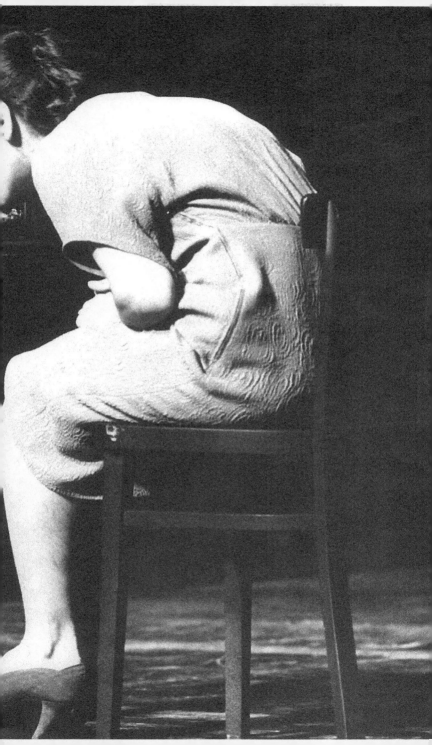

LIST OF ILLUSTRATIONS

Ulli Weiss *Bandoneon* Photo Captions

(The images cover the rehearsal period of *Bandoneon* and its performances with the cast of 1980 and 1981. The captions are always from left to right.)

141	The stage hands come on stage during the show and remove the set – as part of the performance.
142/143	Beatrice Libonati, Hans Dieter Knebel, Heide Tegeder, Arthur Rosenfeld, Malou Airaudo, Jan Minarik
144	Malou Airaudo
145	Malou Airaudo, Dominique Mercy
146	Dominique Mercy
147	Malou Airaudo
148	Dominique Mercy, Malou Airaudo
149	Urs Kaufmann, Meryl Tankard
150/151	Heide Tegeder, Meryl Tankard
152	Nazareth Panadero, Malou Airaudo
153-155	Nazareth Panadero, Meryl Tankard
156-157	Christian Trouillas, Nazareth Panadero
158/159	Urs Kaufmann, Meryl Tankard, Heide Tegeder, Hans Dieter Knebel
160	Dominique Mercy, Malou Airaudo
161	Arthur Rosenfeld, Isabel Ribas Serra
162	Anne Martin
163	Isabel Ribas Serra
164/165	Beatrice Libonati
166	Mechthild Großmann
167	Jan Minarik
168/169	Hans Dieter Knebel, Isabel Ribas Serra, Urs Kaufmann, Nazareth Panadero, Malou Airaudo, Janusz Subicz, Jean-Laurent Sasportes, Heide Tegeder, Meryl Tankard, Arthur Rosenfeld, Anne Martin, Christian Trouillas, Anne Marie Benati, Vivienne Newport, Mechthild Großmann, Beatrice Libonati, Jan Minarik
170/171	Dominique Mercy, Hans Dieter Knebel, Urs Kaufmann, Isabel Ribas Serra, Nazareth Panadero, Janusz Subicz, Malou Airaudo, Jean-Laurent Sasportes
172	Meryl Tankard, Christian Trouillas
173	Dominique Mercy

CHILDHOOD PHOTOS
OF THE ENSEMBLE

– as featured in the programme of
'Bandoneon. A piece by Pina Bausch' (1980)
by the ensemble of the Tanztheater Wuppertal

Hans Pop

schön ist sich
Kaputt zu lachen

It's lovely to laugh oneself silly.

Anne Martin

178

Touched once in Buenos. Aires
Callas' dress from Turandot.

Touched once in Buenos Aires Maria
Callas' dress from Turandot.

Dominique Mercy

Jetzt ist es schon wieder Winter

Once again it is winter.

Anne Marie Benati

*Handmal wünsche ich mir, in einer
Großstadt aufgewachsen zu sein.
Wenn wir nach Italien fahren, hoffe ich,
Frauen zu sehen mit dicken schweren Brüsten.*

Sometimes I wish I'd grown up in a big city.
When we go to Italy, I hope to see women
with fat, heavy breasts.

Urs Kaufmann (on the right)

Deer, when they mate, the male chases
the female for a long time, but when he
catches her, it only lasts 2 or 3 seconds.

Christian Trouillas

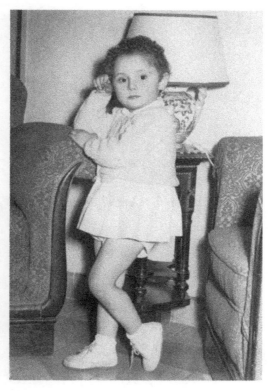

Sie haben mit mir Ihre Zeit nicht verloren.

Time spent with me is not lost.

Nazareth Panadero

Bis morgen ist noch
so lang.

It's so long until tomorrow.

Hans Dieter Knebel

Marion Cito

*Immer die Sonne schien und wir sind
irgendwo hingegangen, hat mich meine Mutter
ausgezogen und nackt in die Sonne gestellt.*

*Always, when the sun shone and we went
somewhere, my mother undressed me and
placed me in the sunshine, naked.*

Janusz Subicz

I NEVER
fiND a MAN
WHO DANTES
TANGO
LIKE MY FATHER

I never
find a man
who dances
tango
like my father.

Malou Airaudo

Gralf-Edzard Habben (on the right)

What about saying "Hi" to me

What about saying 'Hi' to me.

Meryl Tankard

Ich wußte nicht, daß bestimmte Tiere, zum Beispiel Schweine, so Geschlechtsteile in Ringel-form haben. Als ich das im Zoo zum ersten Mal sah, wußte ich überhaupt nicht, was das war.

I didn't know that the genitals of certain animals, pigs for example, are corkscrew-shaped. When I saw one for the first time in a zoo, I had no idea what it was.

Mechthild Großmann

Täuzer tragen dicke Socken,
weil sie warm sind

*Dancers like thick socks because they're
warm.*

Jan Minarik

Schön ist apple - crumble

Schöner ist blackberry - and - apple crumble

am Schönsten ist blackberry - and - apple crumble
and custard

Apple crumble is lovely.
Blackberry and apple crumble is lovelier.
But the loveliest is blackberry and apple crumble
with custard.

Vivienne Newport

192

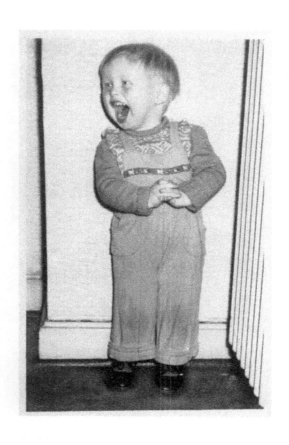

Matthias Burkert

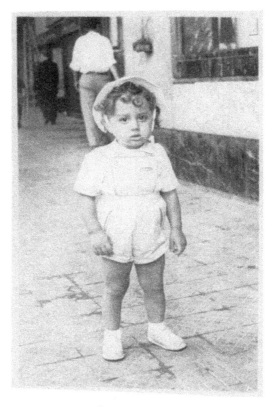

Es gibt ein alte frau die hinter dem piano tee trinkt

There is an old woman who drinks tea
behind the piano.

Jean-Laurent Sasportes

Alle Goldhamster die es gibt, stammen
von einem einzigen Elternpaar ab.
Ein israelischer Zoologe hat sie um 1930
aus der syrischen Wüste mitgebracht.

All golden hamsters are descended
from one single parental pair. An Israeli
zoologist brought them back from the
Syrian Desert in 1930.

Heide Tegeder

Ich vermiße, morgens die Flasche nach draußen stellen für den Milchmann.

It's on with the show! Away we go!

I miss putting out the bottle for the
milkman in the morning.
It's on with the show! Away we go!

Arthur Rosenfeld

Ich finde Tango gut für einen
schönen alten Herrn Kennen lernen,
Leidenschaft fühlen und auch
Nein sagen.
   In Holland, I like very much
this big windows without courtains,
that you can see the people
inside.

I think tango is good for meeting a nice old
man, feeling passion, and also saying no.
In Holland, I like very much this big
windows without curtains, that you can
see the people inside.

Isabel Ribas Serra

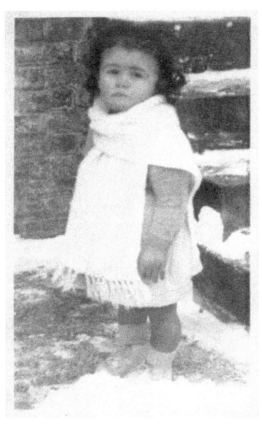

es ist so schön wenn die Sonne menchmal rauskommt in Deutschland

It's so lovely when the sun sometimes comes out in Germany.

Beatrice Libonati

Raimund Hoghe

Pina Bausch

B A N D O N E O N

Ein Stück von Pina Bausch

Inszenierung und Choreographie: **Pina Bausch**
Bühne: **Gralf-Edzard Habben**
Kostüme: **Marion Cito**
Dramaturgie: **Raimund Hoghe**
Mitarbeit: **Matthias Burkert/Hans Pop**
Technische Leitung: **Rolf Bachmann**

mit

Malou Airaudo
Anne Marie Benati
Lutz Förster
Mechthild Grossmann
Urs Kaufmann
Hans Dieter Knebel
Beatrice Libonati
Anne Martin
Dominique Mercy
Jan Minarik
Vivienne Newport
Nazareth Panadero
Isabel Ribas Serra
Arthur Rosenfeld
Jean-Laurent Sasportes
Janusz Subicz
Meryl Tankard
Heide Tegeder
Christian Trouillas

Musik: Tangos

Trainingsleiter: Jean Cebron/Dominique Mercy, Pianist: Matthias
Burkert, Inspizient: Herbert Görsch, Bühneneinrichtung:
Pip Flood-Murphy, Lichtgestaltung: Houshmand Mazloum, Requisiten:
Günther Fränzel, Masken: Heinz Dildey, Ton: Klaus Grimm/Horst
Kersten, Leiterin der Kostümabteilung: Renate Eichberg, Werkstätten-
leitung: Leo Haase

Spieldauer ca. 3 Stunden - Eine Pause

6. Januar 1981

Cast list of Bandoneon – *a 6 January 1981*
performance at the Wuppertal Opera House

A PORTRAIT OF RAIMUND HOGHE

An interview by Katalin Trencsényi

Katalin Trencsényi:

How did your professional career start?

Raimund Hoghe:

I come from Wuppertal. After completing my school in the late 1960s, I started working for the newspaper *Westdeutsche Zeitung.* Journalism was an obvious choice for me, because at the end of my schooling I was already writing and had articles published. When I was at school I also had a go at acting, and performed in the theatre of Wuppertal as an 'extra', playing very small parts, for example in Shakespeare pieces, but I knew that I would never be a professional actor, so I opted for writing. From my early days as a journalist I chose social themes and culture: presenting the life of social minorities and writing about fine art and theatre. I also worked for a cultural program at the radio Westdeutscher Rundfunk, mostly doing theatre reviews. Later I went freelance, writing for *Die Zeit* and for *Theater heute,* and continued working for the radio.

KT:

How did you hear about Pina Bausch?

RH:

In the late 1970s I moved to Düsseldorf, and in the Schauspielhaus I saw for the first time a piece by Pina Bausch. It was her choreography, an interpretation of *Blaubart (Bluebeard)*, and I was very impressed. So I decided to go to Wuppertal to see the premiere of her other work, *Kontakthof*, and that too I liked very much.

Around the same time, in 1979, *Theater heute* asked me to write a portrait of Pina. I interviewed her and watched some rehearsals of *Arien (Arias)*. Then I penned the essay, which became the first of many articles I wrote about her work. Later it appeared in my book about her: *Pina Bausch, Tanztheatergeschichten*.[1]

I wanted to follow her work and asked Pina to allow me to sit in the rehearsals of her next piece, *Keuschheitslegende (The Legend of Chastity)*. This was a rare privilege to allow someone, especially a critic, to follow her work for a longer period of time. She said yes, and in exchange asked me to write something for their programme for the premiere of the piece. She warned me that she didn't want too much spelt out about the intention of the work or be too explanatory or render any meaning to the piece that the audience was about to see. I agreed with this approach completely. So I wrote a diary about the rehearsals. She and her partner, and ingenious set designer for the Tanztheater Wuppertal, Rolf Borzik very much liked my essay. (I always mention Pina and Rolf together, because it was a very close collaboration, a strong artistic and personal relationship between them.)

When we did *Keuschheitslegende*, Rolf was already very ill, and a few weeks after the premiere he died of leukaemia. Gradually I became close friends with Pina and carried on coming to the rehearsals. Consequently, when she made her next piece, *1980 – Ein Stück von Pina Bausch (1980 – a Piece by Pina Bausch)*, I was acknowledged on the programme as her dramaturg. Then I remained with the ensemble and worked as their dramaturg for a decade, until 1989. It was an organic development, from a friendship to becoming her dramaturg. But it was always inseparable for Pina: life and the artistic work – they were always connected throughout.

KT:

Did she declare at any point that from now on you would be the ensemble's dramaturg?

RH:

No. She always had assistants who came from the ensemble, but working with her was a collaboration, and these roles always evolved. Before I joined the company, Ille Chamier worked as some sort of dramaturgical assistant with Pina from 1975 to 1978. They knew each other from the Folkwangschule. This collaboration resulted in a photo album accompanied by poetic reflections about Bausch's work, a co-creation between photographer Ulli Weiss and Ille Chamier: *Setz dich hin und lächle.* [2]

Some of Pina's assistants were dancers (Hans Pop, Marion Cito) who carried on performing with the company on the stage as well as helping Pina. But apart from bigger pieces, like her Macbeth-project, *Er nimmt sie an der Hand und führt sie in das Schloß, die andern folgen* (*He takes her by the hand and leads her into the castle, the others follow*), when she got assigned assistants from the Schauspielhaus Bochum, Pina didn't employ outsiders to assist her.

KT:

The company not only worked together but almost lived together, it seems to me.

RT:

Living in Wuppertal is not like living in London or Paris! There are not many good places to go to eat out. Similarly, there isn't a huge choice of what to do or what to see. And this contributed in a way to create the ensemble.

The fact, that at the beginning the town didn't accept our work, and we felt that they were in many ways against us, served to glue the company together, in a kind of act of resistance, which also fuelled the work.

Being part of the Tanztheater Wuppertal meant being part of a community, being Pina's 'family'. Our professional and private lives were intertwined.

After the rehearsals we stayed and hung out together. We went to eat at a local restaurant, near the rehearsal space, the Lichtburg. During dinner Pina couldn't stop thinking about the work, so she took a piece of paper out, and the discussion carried on, and people stayed until long into the night talking about the piece we were working on. And if our conversations continued past the time when the last train was gone, we slept in Pina's flat in Fingscheid Street.

KT:

Where did the company used to go to hang out?

RT:

We often went to a very simple Greek restaurant, called Delphi, just around the corner of the Lichtburg. Sometimes we ate at the Moevenpick restaurant, also very close to our rehearsal space, or at the Café du Congo in Elberfeld. There wasn't a huge choice!

KT:

When you became the dramaturg of the Tanztheater Wuppertal, were you aware of the fact that you were the first dance dramaturg in the world?

RH:

No. It wasn't that kind of official appointment. I was very much connected to Pina by our relations, our tastes, the similarities between her thinking about staging things and my way of writing, what we thought about structuring our work etc. I was interested in working with Pina. It was a personal relationship and an artistic relationship.

KT:

Were you employed by the company?

Pina Bausch and Raimund Hoghe at the Lichtburg (1989)
Photography: © Detlef Erler

RH:

I was not employed to work for the theatre full time; I only had contracts for the productions. In those days the Tanztheater Wuppertal was part of the Wuppertaler Bühnen and was not an independent company; it belonged to the city. Besides, I also continued to work as a journalist.

KT:

The fact that Bausch acknowledged your contribution to the work as a dance dramaturg led to profound changes in the profession in Europe in the 1980s.

RH:

Yes, but at that time we didn't feel that. It was a freelance commission and wasn't well paid. It alone wouldn't have sustained me.

Equally, it was important for me to keep my independence. During this decade with the Tanztheater Wuppertal I hadn't given up my career in journalism: I continued writing articles and published several books. When I stayed at Pina's flat, we often talked about my work as a writer and not about the dance theatre.

KT:

How did you divide your time between Düsseldorf and Wuppertal?

RH:

I commuted to Wuppertal from Düsseldorf usually two to three times a week, or more if I was needed to watch something and respond to. However, in a way I remained someone 'coming from the outside'.

KT:

How did you regard your role as the dramaturg of Pina Bausch?

RH:

We understood each other very well: we had similar ideas and the same taste. Once Pina said about herself: 'I watch people how they behave, what they do'. I did the same with my writing. This was the common interest that brought us together.

Sometimes Pina was insecure. Even though she was a great artist, she had her doubts. And when she said, 'Oh, I don't know whether this is too long or boring!', I was there to reassure her.

I wanted to support her, so she could do what she wanted. This is how I understood my role as her dramaturg. It was a deep friendship.

Pina didn't ask people to come to the rehearsals to give comments; she made the pieces she wanted to see. And I liked this very much about her. This applies to her early years, the decade when we worked together. Later this changed somewhat.

KT:

How long did you rehearse a new piece for?

RH:

Usually for two months. But some pieces, like *Café Müller* or *1980* took a shorter time.

Pina Bausch working (1980)
Photography: © Raimund Hoghe

KT:

How did you work with Pina Bausch?

RH:

Although I worked with Pina on the *Keuschheitslegende* in 1979, our first full work was *1980,* a piece that came about from the shock of the death of her partner, and the company's designer, Rolf Borzik. Apart from spending some time with the ensemble in the rehearsal room, I created the programme for the premiere. I collated selected images from Rolf's drawings and sketches, accompanied by a list of tag words from the rehearsals: instructions and questions from Pina to the dancers during the work.

KT:

Those words: 'what would you normally do alone', 'a very beautiful moment of a fairy tale', 'behaviour of bees', 'traumatic moments', 'this is very funny', 'mourn', 'children prayers', 'seven ways to say "I'm fine"', etc. – even in their dense and enigmatic way, say something important about the piece and its themes...

RH:

We had no text, just questions and questions that Pina took into the rehearsal room. During our work I noted down the questions (more than a hundred) she asked the dancers, as well as their answers.

KT:

What was her creative process like?

RH:

She didn't know where the piece would go when she started. Maybe she had a desire inside. In the case of *1980* it was a feeling of loss. The title is a date because this was the year when Rolf died, but Pina didn't want to make it explicit that she created this piece for Rolf. However, the title continues: *Ein Stück von Pina Bausch – A piece of Pina Bausch.* And there is a double entendre here, meaning that this is not only a piece she created but is also a piece from Pina, as she was saying farewell to Rolf who was clearly part of her. This was the first and only time when Pina mentioned herself in the title – in other works the line 'Ein Stück von Pina Bausch' remained a subtitle.

KT:

This gesture is more than just claiming ownership. It is emphasising her relationship to these pieces. To remain with your analogy: if the Tanztheater Wuppertal was Bausch's family, these pieces were her children. So how did these 'children' come about?

RH:

The ensemble rehearsed in the morning and in the evening in a disused cinema, the Lichtburg. And in between rehearsals Pina stayed there – sometimes alone, sometimes with some dancers or assistants.

The dancers turned up in the morning after the ballet training, with their coffees, settled down, and Pina put her questions to them, maybe five or six for one session. The dancers responded, and those answers were noted down, because everything was important and could become potent for Pina. She was very clear about what she felt or how she worked, but she never gave any explanations before or during the rehearsals (only maybe after). Pina once said, 'I don't know what the result will be when I ask a question. If I knew, I wouldn't ask the question.'

Then later, after this first period of the work, she took out her list, and asked people to repeat those things that she liked. And some dancers could reproduce them very well, whereas others were not great at doing so. This also reduced the material available to work with.

Pina didn't have a masterplan or a structure beforehand, it all came about during the rehearsals, by trying out things and seeing how it would work if we would put this next to this. She would also try out different music – although, the music came much later.

KT:

First you created the material then progressed by reducing and shaping it. Shall we to talk more about the first stage, when the dancers were generating material by responding to Pina Bausch's questions? What was your role during this stage?

RH:

Just watching and writing down the questions and answers. I brought Pina texts and music that became part of the performance. So did the dancers. I also talked to the dancers about the issues I was writing about those days for the journal (social issues, HIV etc.). For

Bandoneon, for instance, we created a project, whereby the company brought in their childhood photos, and we gave a line from the rehearsals to every photo.

KT:

These photos with the accompanying texts became the programme notes for the show. Alongside the dancers' pictures, it includes the photos of both Pina Bausch and you as a child. Pina Bausch is cradling a doll, whereas you are holding a Schultüte (a cone full of small gifts and sweets German children receive when they start school). It is very personal and revealing about yourselves.

RH:

Pina didn't want to have much text in the programme, and the idea of including our childhood photos that we used for the rehearsals appealed to her.

KT:

What did you note down during the rehearsals?

RH:

What I saw, what they said, and sometimes thoughts or ideas that occurred to me during the rehearsals. For instance, I suggested the famous Judy Garland song, *Over the Rainbow,* to be used in *1980* twice: once in a version sung by the young Garland at the beginning of her career, and later in the piece when we hear it again, it is a different recording, sung by her when she was old. It fitted in the piece very well.

When you got to the next stage of the work, selecting the material, did she consult you on this?

RH:

No. She knew what she wanted. Later I could suggest how to order or structure things, or perhaps I remembered what someone did which Pina hadn't included in her list, and recommended her to use that bit.

KT:

Once she had selected potential building blocks of the performance in the making that resonated with her, and then asked the dancers to repeat them, what happened?

RH:

We went through those, and Pina further reduced the selection. Maybe some things could not be repeated any longer, or maybe she didn't like them for the second time. In this way she could eliminate some of the ideas, and narrow down the focus.

KT:

What followed this filtering process?

RH:

Then Pina tried to connect these different moments to make the whole piece.

During the period when the dancers offered 'answers' to her questions, Pina wrote down everything on her papers. At this stage she began to move these pieces of paper, putting them next to each other, grouping them in different ways, repeating them etc. and trying out these ideas for creating a structure with the company. She moved forward inch by inch.

KT:

How did you find connections between these smaller units?

RH:

By trying out what could come one after the other. What would continue the feeling, or on the contrary, what could contrast with it. As Pina noted once: the piece was growing from the inside to the outside. She had a desire inside that she couldn't express in words, so she did it on the stage with people.

KT:

Did the ensemble help her at this stage?

RH:

Yes. When creating *1980*, Meryl Tankard was very good at offering ideas about how to connect her material, or making suggestions about her costumes.

Jan Minarik was one of the most important collaborators: he was excellent at observing the work and coming up with suggestions. He watched a lot, and therefore often entered the stage quite late in the piece. He too also contributed with ideas for his often strange costumes.

Jan once said in an interview that when he was watching the other dancers, he thought about the movements he was about to contribute: 'Maybe I could do this not as a comment but as a contrast.'

Raimund Hoghe, Mechthild Großmann, Jan Minarik and Pina Bausch at the rehearsal of Two Cigarettes in the Dark *(1985) Photography: Ulli Weiss, © Pina Bausch Foundation*

Nowadays when I make my own work, I often think of this quote of Jan. Because he had a special presence on the stage: disturbing sometimes but very necessary.

KT:

Pina Bausch was known for carrying on working on her pieces after the premiere. Did you play any part in this?

RH:

I went to see every performance. Usually after the premiere Pina only further trimmed the pieces, or cut out scenes for instance. Although in *Nelken* (*Carnations*) she made a big change after the premiere: originally it was a very long piece with two intervals. She cut it back until she got rid of the breaks.

KT:

How did Bandoneon *come about?*

RH:

The inspiration came from the Tanztheater Wuppertal's South American tour during the summer of 1980. The company took three pieces there: *Kontakthof, Café Müller* and *Le Sacre du printemps (The Rite of Spring).*

It was a very important tour for Pina. There she met Ronald Kay, who became her partner (and the father of her son); and she was also very impressed by the music and the dance of tango. For instance, the photos on the wall of the set of *Bandoneon* mainly came from these cafés in South America. Or the choice of music: unlike in her other pieces, where the music was eclectic, in *Bandoneon* Pina only used music from South America.

With the loss of Rolf, the company was deprived of their designer, hence for the next few pieces Pina was experimenting with commissioning other set designers, until she settled in working with Peter Pabst. For *Bandoneon* the set was designed by Gralf-Edzard Habben.

I documented the way we developed this piece in my book of the same title,[3] and Pina was very happy that the process was preserved. In those days the Tanztheater Wuppertal's work wasn't followed to the same extent as later, therefore my writings are an important documentation of the period, and Pina's way of working.

KT:

You stayed with the Tanztheater Wuppertal for a decade. Why was it important for you to work with them?

RH:

It was really like a family for me and I liked working with Pina. I admired her unique artistic process and also I loved working with the dancers, who were great artists. I worked with them on seven new dance pieces (including *Walzer, Nelken, Viktor,* and *Ahnen*), and a film *Die Klage der Kaiserin (The Plaint of the Empress).*

KT:

How would you describe your period with Pina Bausch?

RH:

I think that the time from the late 1970s till the late 1980s was a very important artistic period in the life of the Tanztheater Wuppertal. They created some of their seminal works then, and there were some strong personalities and great artists in the ensemble (Jan Minarik, Jo Ann Endicott, Dominique Mercy, Meryl Tankard etc.).

I must admit, I prefer the work that Pina made in the 1970s and the 1980s. To me those pieces where she was bold, strong and uncompromising are the best: her Brecht-Weill evening, *Die Seben Todsünden* *(Seven Deadly Sins of the Petty Bourgeoisie* and *Don't Be Afraid), Le Sacre du printemps, Blaubart,* her *Macbeth* paraphrase, *Kontakthof, Café Müller,* and *Arien (Arias).* These dance pieces were very theatrical, and impressed many theatre professionals. This was also the time when she gained international recognition as a remarkable choreographer. Robert Wilson, Luc Bondy and other great theatre makers came to Wuppertal to see Pina's work, and Heiner Müller wrote a long essay about her.[4]

KT:

Today people seem to have forgotten how hard it was for Pina Bausch to get her work acknowledged locally. I read about how in the 1970s she was harassed by the Wuppertal authorities…

RH:

Even in the 1980s she wasn't acknowledged by the local theatre goers. I remember *Kontakthof* being performed in the Wuppertal Opera House, with hardly sixty people (filling only two rows!) sitting in the auditorium at the beginning of the performance, and only half of them staying till the end. Those who left during the show let

The ensemble rehearsing Bandoneon *at the Lichtburg (1980)*
Photography: © Raimund Hoghe

the door bang on their way out just to demonstrate their anger and frustration with our work.

Before the mid-1980s you could always get a ticket for Pina's work in Wuppertal! Of course this has changed a lot, once she became world famous.

KT:

Why did you leave the Tanztheater Wuppertal?

RH:

Pina's film was the last production I was involved in. It was a very different work. Unusually for Pina, she had a three year break from creating a new piece. She was exhausted from work. *Die Klage der Kaiserin* was a very strong work of hers, lots of suffering and pain went into the filming. But it wasn't a commercial success, and for Pina, who by then had received international acknowledgement, it was a blow.

This was also a time when somehow a phase in the ensemble's life came to a natural end, and Pina had to deal with losses. Just after the filming the cameraman had died. Many people, important dancers and long-time collaborators (for instance, Anne Martin, who was very close to Pina: she took over her role in *Café Müller*) left the company. I too began to feel that it was time to go – with Pina revising her older pieces, there was no new work for me. I was also encouraged to do my own artistic work.

We began to drift away. I embarked on a collaboration with someone else, whereas Pina started to look for a new direction in her work. I wasn't involved in her next piece, but she rang me for my opinion on *Palermo Palermo*. I still came often to see the performances in Wuppertal, until, gradually, I stopped.

KT:

How did Pina Bausch take your departure?

RH:

My relationship with Pina was a very close friendship. But by the late 1980s, it was time for me for change. She understood this, but I don't think she forgave me for this. Regrettably she never came to see any of my performances. She found it difficult to accept when people left the company.

KT:

Do you think that later she has become the victim of her own success? And once her work was accepted as mainstream, a certain style was expected from her?

RH:

Forty years is a long time in the life of a dance company. Relationships change. The dancers change, either become 'tired' or leave – only a few remained from the core ensemble. And I found Pina's later works completely different, less strong, compared to her earlier work, and in a way more artificial and populist. I found Pina repeating herself and her previous artistic choices, as well as her dancers repeating the same roles through the decades, without having a chance to accept their age on the stage and perform a different role.

I don't know how Pina felt later in her life, I only remember what she said about her work. She said that when she was doing these dark and painful pieces, she wasn't depressed, on the contrary: she felt very good. Because you can say very heavy and sad things when you are stable and you are able to look at these difficult topics with a distance. Whereas when she was creating her happier pieces, she felt sad inside, that's why she needed to create something cheerful to look at. By watching Pina's last few works, one can decide how she must have felt in her last years…

KT:

How did your career as a dancer-choreographer start?

RH:

The editing of Pina's film took a very long time, and people in the ensemble started to feel a bit restless. One of the dancers, Mark Sieczkarek got an opportunity from the Folkwang Tanzstudio in Essen, and Pina (who was still the artistic director of the Tanzstudio) agreed to this. I became dramaturg of Mark's solo piece, *Forbidden Fruit.* This led to working with other dancers and actors (for instance, I worked with Ricardo Bittencourt on *Vento*), then gradually I began creating my own pieces for dancers and actors.

In 1992 I started to collaborate with the visual artist Luca Giacomo Schulte on my first solo piece, *Verdi Prati,* for the dancer Rodolpho Leoni, and this is the point from when I count my career as a choreographer. This artistic collaboration with Luca has remained ever since. In

1994 I created my first solo performance *Meinwärts* for the Hebbel Theater Berlin, and from then on I appear in every piece I make.

At that time when you started your career as a dancer and choreographer you were 43 years old. Why did this change happen?

RH:

It wasn't a substantial change, only formal: from writing words on paper I switched to writing with bodies on the stage – but the subject remained the same: portraits of people. I had this strong urge to talk via the medium of dance about issues that I found important and couldn't express otherwise.

I explained this in my essay, *Writing with words and bodies*: 'Between writing with words and writing with bodies – ultimately there is no difference for me. Only that the body of the author is visible on stage and is part of the writing. It's not only words that can write a text.' My first choreographies were solo pieces for dancers. They were the portraits of these dancers, and I was 'writing' their stories.

KT:

Being a dancer is a very exposed position. How did you find it?

RH:

When I talk about this, I usually borrow a phrase from the late film director, Pier Paolo Pasolini: 'throwing the body into the fight'.

One of the last photos made of him in 1975 (near the untimely end of his life) depicts the middle-aged Pasolini posing naked. I was very impressed how bravely he presented his body. Similarly, the French writer, Hervé Guibert who died of AIDS, filmed himself going into the water naked. And this too is a striking image: his skinny, ill, vulnerable body. And it has a very powerful message about beauty, ageing, illness and death.

These people gave me the courage to put my body, 'that does not comply with the norm', on stage. Nevertheless, the stage in my very first pieces was always very dark. The light was dimmed, sometimes only candles lit the space, and I was wearing a dark suit, my body was often invisible, I was almost hiding. I only started to use bright lights in recent years to present myself.

KT:

What did you take away from that decade working with Pina Bausch?

RH:

That she made pieces that she wanted to see. And that you can only listen to your own inner voice. And how important the form was for her: not just to put raw feelings on the stage. It's not the surface.

The relevance of the presence of the dancers: all the pieces Pina created were made possible only because of the collaboration of the ensemble of the Tanztheater Wuppertal. One cannot emphasise enough the dancers' contribution to these performances.

From Pina I also learnt how she was with the dancers in the rehearsal room. That she never interrupted anyone, she didn't judge, she was just open to see – so people were very free. And this is very important to me to give the people I work with the feeling that they are free and accepted.

KT:

In what way is your work as a choreographer different from the work of Pina Bausch?

RT:

I work with fewer dancers than Pina, I am not interested in video projections, and I have a different image than hers for the women of today.

The image she created in her later periods of portraying women: wearing high heels and evening dresses, letting their hair down, doing their little power games between man and women – I don't do that. The women in my choreographies are portrayed otherwise. I also deliberately choose to work with older dancers.

Our dramaturgy is different: our sense of the beginning and end, and the use of repetitions. Our sense of time on the stage is dissimilar. There is an anecdote of Pina saying, 'Oh, I can't ask Raimund about the length of this piece because nothing is ever too long for him, and he would just say, "Take your time!"'

When I replace a dancer in an already made choreography with another, unlike Pina, I don't want the new dancer to repeat exactly the previous dancer's moves. I enjoy the way a new personality changes the piece.

KT:

Is it because – contrary to belief – Pina Bausch created roles and characters for the dancers in her pieces, whereas you use the dancers' actual personality as their stage persona?

RH:

I work with the dancer's personality differently than Pina did. I take into account for instance the fact that these people mature and change with time. This is the reason why I don't keep the same pieces for too long in the repertoire. It is different when you dance the same role when you are twenty-eight or when you are fifty-eight. Besides, those pieces were made at a time when I was interested in a particular problem.

KT:

Do you mind that despite your own career as a choreographer, your name is so strongly associated with Pina Bausch's?

RH:

No. It's really not a problem for me. What is a problem is how many people try to hang on to her name claiming that they worked closely with her or played an important part in her life. I don't need to live from her reputation, as before joining her company as a dramaturg, I was well known as a writer – a career that I never gave up. It was only one decade in my life, the 1980s when I worked for Pina.

KT:

In your essay, 'Writing with words and bodies' you write that dramaturgy for you is how one gets from A to B.

RH:

When you go from one point to another on the stage and you don't have to stop and think about it, but it comes naturally, that's when it is the right movement, built on the previous one. If there isn't a natural flow in there, then I have to change it (replace the music, introduce text, whatever is needed) because it shows that something is wrong with the piece's dramaturgy.

KT:

What is dramaturgy for you?

RH:

To build a clear structure. It is how time, space and rhythm come together in a piece. The 'empty' space that connects two points. That charged space that holds the work together is very important for me. That's why I like to perform in big spaces.

KT:

As a dancer and choreographer where do you place yourself in the contemporary dance landscape?

RH:

In Germany the desire to label everything goes back to historical reasons. But I refuse to be labelled – even though these tags (old, dementia, gay, disabled, historical, political, Jewish etc.) bring money to a company or a production.

I do what I feel I have to do: to share with the audience beauty, the quality of music, the quality of the dancers, and our history. These are my main themes.

History features in all my pieces – even in my solo about Judy Garland, *An Evening with Judy*, there is something about the Third Reich: a scene from her 1961 film, *Judgment at Nuremberg*.

The reason I do this kind of work is because I don't see it elsewhere on the stage, therefore I feel that I have to make it. Today not many people talk about beauty, or personal history and personal memory connected with our collective history. My work is never about one person only.

Earlier in my career I wrote many portraits – of famous people as well as ordinary people. One of my favourite ones was about a cleaning woman, *An ordinary woman I am*, published in *Die Zeit*. Her story reflected the lives of many other working-class women, not only cleaners, but waitresses, concierges, and shop assistants. Accordingly, in my choreographies one piece shows the stories of many other people.

KT:

What are your influences as a choreographer?

RH:

Music, the personality of the dancers, the time we live in, and beauty.

I think music has the greatest power. With music I can achieve things that I can't do otherwise physically. And it has a healing quality that I also use in my work.

My work has always been inspired by people. Now that I 'write' with bodies on the stage, it is inspired by the dancers I'm working with, and the beauty they present me with.

KT:

Do you choose the music first, when you work? Do you start from a musical structure?

RH:

No. Sometimes there is an interest in someone or I like a piece of music.

My first solo, *Meinwärts,* was about Joseph Schmidt, a great Jewish tenor who was exiled by the Nazis. The idea came through Luca [Giacomo Schulte] and his grandmother who talked about him. Then I read about his life, and I was impressed by it: Schmidt was a world-famous star with an incredible voice. Apart from the fascination with his art and life, I also found more personal connections between him and I. Physically, for instance: he was very small, just over 1.5 metres, therefore a career on stage was impossible for him. Or the arguments fascists used against the Jews (and consequently against Schmidt) reminded me of the 1990s when many people died of AIDS, and it was similar rhetoric against gay people. So I took the biography of Schmidt to say something about the rising voice of fascism and about the scars of history in the present Germany.

Maria Callas captivated me by her incredible voice and success, and the contrast of her end: dying alone in her Paris apartment, being left without friends and having no money. So that's how my second solo piece about a singer, *36, Avenue Georges Mandel* came about in 2007.

An Evening with Judy (2013) was created because ever since my childhood I was a big fan of Judy Garland and loved many songs by her. I was also captivated by her destiny: having been abused by her parents to take drugs and pills to work as a child. In my preceding work, *Cantatas* (2012), I had a very strong moment evoking Garland, and that prompted the idea to develop it into a piece about her. It also fitted in the series of my solo works about famous singers.

In my other works, like *Pas de Deux* (2011), there is a variety of different genres of music that I use. And it just comes. I don't plan.

For each choreography I discover new music, new singers, or I discover a new interpretation of the same song. I like very much the idea that singers sing and record the same piece at different times of their career, so, inevitably, they interpret it differently.

KT:

You used these different recordings in An Evening with Judy...

RH:

Yes, but it's not at all about my CD collection! I also research the biography of the singers whose music I use, I look up the translations of the lyrics, if it's in a language I

Raimund Hoghe performing Meinwärts *(1994)*
Photography: © *Rosa Frank*

don't understand, I want to know what the song is about, because the lyrics are important.

KT:

Looking back at your oeuvre of over twenty years' work as a choreographer, which pieces do you consider as the most important ones?

RH:

All are important – in a way, it's like being a parent: you can't say which of your children are more important to you. Each of them has different qualities. Maybe at the beginning my work was less strong than it is now, but at the time they were also very powerful; whereas now I have more possibilities.

I like my old pieces. But I stop performing them after a while, because I change. There are some pieces though, for instance, *Lettere amorose*, a solo I created in 1999, I wouldn't mind revisiting, because its theme is very timely today: it's about refugees, people escaping from Africa, children dying as stowaways on the way to Europe.

KT:

Your work is a variation and a development of certain themes. Do you regard your oeuvre this way?

RH:

Every artist has some themes they are interested in. On stage I am not interested in violence. Because violence on stage is never real, you don't really kill someone on stage, it's fake. Whereas love on stage can be real. Relationships that you develop on the stage can be real.

I am not interested in virtuosity – how high someone can jump etc. – what is important to me are: intimate things, simple movements, and the personalities of my dancers.

KT:

What themes are you interested in as an artist?

RH:

Life and death! *[laughs]* Beauty, music, and what can help people to survive. It is important for me to offer people quality to counteract what the media offer to people. I believe that people are hungry to see something different from that. To freely quote Maria Callas: the need is huge for people to show what they fight for and what they live for.

KT:

In your works, alongside beauty the theme of destruction and death also appears…

RH:

I get quite angry about the phenomenon that people behave as if they would live forever. They plan so much ahead in the future, as if death would not exist, at the same time they forget to be in the present.

KT:

This also appears in your choreography, to bring us into the present, slowing down time, to create a different, almost ritualistic passage of time.

RH:

I would like to offer the opportunity that the members of the audience would connect with themselves in a deeper level during the performance, and maybe feel or think differently after the show than before. If they can let it go. That's what theatre is for. Because the music connects you with the centre of your self, where you can encounter yourself, your thoughts, your dreams, your fears; and if you have the time to experience these, afterwards, hopefully, you can feel better.

KT:

In a way you are working against the current practice of presenting incomplete or simultaneous stories, or showing the polyphony of actions on the stage. Your work seems to be minimalist, complete and simple.

RT:

These are all interesting things to watch, but I am not interested in them as an artist, because one can find this in movies and everywhere. I like the stage empty. And it's more and more empty in my works. I wouldn't call it minimalism, it is more reduced to simplicity. It is very similar to the way children play: being in the moment.

KT:

And it is very much charged with energy...

RT:

Yes. And for the children this monotony is not boring. They can play with something for a very long time, and remain very involved.

KT:

Once you said 'I don't have a technique but a strong sense of form.' Where does this sense of form come from?

RH:

It came through the work. When I was working as a writer, I always tried to be very clear. Chekhov said that it is not important to write good lines, what is important is to cut the bad lines. Pina did something similar. When I worked as her dramaturg, we were looking for the same: to cut it back to what it is necessary, to reduce the work to its essence.

KT:

You are not interested in virtuosity but in the intensity of the little movement. Why?

RH:

Because it is enough. And for me it is more interesting when I can't explain the power of a simple, little movement. Why is it so fascinating? Why is it so strong? If someone can jump high like crazy, the explanation is in the virtuosity of the movement, but why is it so powerful if someone just slowly lifts up his/her arm? Of course, it is connected to spirituality, even if what I do is not labelled as spiritual theatre.

Songs for Takashi *(2015)*
L-R: Takashi Ueno, Raimund Hoghe
Photography: © Rosa Frank

KT:

How do you achieve this intensity, this essence of movement?

RH:

It comes from the quality of the dancers I work with. For instance, Takashi [Ueno] can connect very well with the music. Each rehearsal he wants to feel something, he wants to go into the music, and he flies far away with it, and although he doesn't talk about his thinking, I can follow his journey.

KT:

You tend to navigate towards alternative venues...

RH:

I don't think so. I just like creating work, or even just performing work, for different spaces and not only for black box. We performed *An Evening with Judy* in a traditional Kabuki theatre in Japan – and it looked very beautiful there. The performance's connection with Kabuki got amplified there.

KT:

How do you create your work?

RH:

Peter Brook said once that at the rehearsals you have to create an atmosphere where things can happen. You have to be open to this.

I play music. Maybe there is an idea or a theme to start with. Like for *Quartet* (2014) we started with Schubert's *String Quartet (Death and the Maiden)*, and four dancers. The dancers responded to it, the work grew, and things gradually came together with the movement and the costumes.

When I work with the dancers, I don't ask questions like Pina, I just play music and see how they react. If they can connect with the music, I'll work with that piece of music, if not, I have to find another music. Very often what happens is that we discover something and it starts growing and growing.

KT:

Jonathan Burrows calls this method when he asks the dancers to improvise and the choreography is gradually developed and edited from that material: 'cut and paste'.

RH:

I don't call what the dancers do 'improvisation': they do something *with* the music, they *connect* with the music. Therefore for my work the film documentation of every rehearsal is very important. But somehow my experience (and the dancers tend to agree with me on this) is that what the dancers do for the first time is the best, because then they don't think about what to do and how to do, they just listen. Later I make a list with time codes for each song, and if necessary we can watch it together.

KT:

It sounds like a very collaborative process.

RH:

Except that I choose the whole theme for the piece, I bring the music, the costumes, and I make the decision on what to keep from their recorded movements. But they bring their personalities to it. And this is very similar to Pina's method, because there was also no discussion when she worked. What I learnt from her was that during the rehearsals she never interrupted the dancers, never commented on their work, she just wrote everything down. Today it's easier, because I record everything with a camera.

KT:

There are two artists with whom your working relationship can be considered dramaturgical. I have in mind Rosa Frank, photographer, and Luca Giacomo Schulte, designer and the only witness of your rehearsals.

RH:

Rosa only comes at a later stage of the work, near the end, before the premiere, and helps to find strong, iconic images for the work, that go on the promotional material and the programme.

Luca's role is different. For my earlier work he used to design the set. It was always connected to his work as an artist, so (just like his artwork) the design was always very simple, with only a few objects in the space. Luca is also the one who records the rehearsals on film, and sometimes comments on my work. Especially if I dance in my choreography, he draws my attention to moments.

For instance, Luca spotted a movement during the rehearsals of *Pas de Deux* (2011), a scene when Takashi lifts me like in classical ballet, and he suggested that I kept it. From the stage this felt stupid, but when I watched

Raimund Hoghe Quartet *ensemble (2014)*

L-R: Raimund Hoghe, Emmanuel Eggermont, Takashi Ueno,
Ornella Balestra, Yuta Ishikawa, Marion Ballester,
Luca Giacomo Schulte

Photography: © Rosa Frank

back the recording, I realised what Luca meant, so we worked it out properly with Takashi, and now it is part of the piece.

KT:

Once you said: 'Apart from Luca, nobody is there when I rehearse with the dancers. I don't present work in progress to friends to get feedback. I talk to Luca or watch the rehearsals he has filmed.'[5] What are these discussions like?

RH:

I am always in an exchange with Luca, but these are not long discussions. In a way I have to know what I want of the work, so with Luca we talk about its realization. I ask questions from him during the rehearsals about practicalities, whether he agrees with me on something, whether a dancer is able to do something etc. It helps that we have the same taste, we like the same things.

KT:

In the history of modern dance one can also find similar dramaturgical relationships. I am thinking of the collaboration between John Cage and Merce Cunningham, or Pina Bausch and Rolf Borzik. In these dialogue-relationships you can find people working with a choreographer, whose job title may not be dramaturg but they fulfil a dramaturgical role for the production and for the choreographer by questioning (and sometimes challenging) their ideas, being present in the rehearsal room, and being as a partner for their ongoing thinking about the work.

RH:

Indeed. Rolf's work for Pina can be definitely regarded this way: he was an incredibly important contributor to her work. My dramaturgical relationship with Luca is very natural: I have been working with him for more than twenty years now.

KT:

You once said it was easy for you to structure the work – the part of the working process that can be very tricky in contemporary dance. I wonder whether this ease with putting the work together and creating its form is a result of your decades of experience, first as a dramaturg then as a choreographer?

RH:

I have a taste. I know what I'd like to express, what I want to say. When I choose a person to create a piece about (Judy Garland or Maria Callas, for instance), I want to be honest and be respectful to them but also show the vulnerable human being beyond the role of the star. I also want the audience to re-discover a great artist, and see what is behind the fame.

KT:

How does your personal experience find its way into the work?

RH:

It is not only me – it goes through a transformation. It is not my private life on the stage. Sometimes people think something is very personal, and it isn't at all, other times, they don't recognise personal references in my work.

I wrote a book about my mother and her struggles – she was like a female character from an Ödön von Horváth play – and it was written from someone else's position, from 'outside'. It is the same with my choreography. I have a distance to myself. I watch the video. I watch what I do. It is not enough people 'vomiting up' their emotions or getting naked on the stage; I am not interested in this – and this is something that I have in common with Pina. She said: 'You have to find a form for the emotions.' There is emotion I express, but it is through the distance and the form, that makes it possible for me – otherwise it is just kitsch or becomes sentimental. It has to be more than one person's story.

KT:

It is your personal interest and motivation, but it has to find a form through which it can be connected to a more universal theme…

RH:

Yes. Then it will be understood and recognized all over the world. Like the way people responded to my piece about Maria Callas (*36, Avenue Georges Mandel*) in South Korea – they were crying, although they didn't understand the words in the music.

KT:

How do you see your choreography has changed in the past twenty years?

RH:

In the beginning I did only solo pieces, then gradually I started to work with more than one dancer on stage. My choreography always depends on the people I work with. These days I work with very well trained dancers. Some of them are classically trained, others come from contemporary dance. But all are people with strong personalities, and I built my choreographies on them. It was through the dancers that I became interested in working on classical dance pieces. This is how I created *Sacre – The Rite of Spring* (2004), *Swan Lake, 4 Acts* (2005), *Boléro Variations* (2007), and *L'Après-midi…* (2008).

KT:

It is interesting how motifs recur through the pieces in your oeuvre. They are repeated or appear as variations on the same theme, and travel through your works. Why?

RH:

As a child I went to the movies with my grandfather to enjoy something different from reality, to dream something. And these are the two worlds that you can find in all my works: dream and reality. Maybe in the earlier pieces you had either this or that, but now you can find both.

KT:

What is also unique about your work is that you use mature dancers on stage, showing the beauty of the ageing body. In fact, you don't stop dancing at the age of 65.

Raimund Hoghe
Photography: © Rosa Frank

RH:

I regularly work with Ornella Balestra who is in her fifties and with Marion Ballester who is in her forties, and their work is very strong and expressive. What I find problematic is when a dancer has to repeat the same role that was choreographed when they were young. However, if you find a choreographer who can work with your age, considering your maturity and experience – that can be very interesting.

For me it was very important to see the Butoh dancer Kazuo Ohno. He must have been in his late seventies or eighties when I first had the opportunity to experience his work and meet him. I wrote about him several times. Or take Gret Palucca, for instance, she was in her eighties, when we met, lively and still teaching dance in her school in Dresden.

In our Western culture it is very difficult to age or become old, especially for women, as there is a certain image that is expected from them to represent. I think it's a pity.

I don't announce my age on the programme. We don't label my work: 'an ageing body is interesting'. This is another problematic issue of our society that we want to put a label, one single label on things.

KT:

Your works are challenging our Western concept of beauty and our society's view on the body, and promote a different paradigm of seeing an ageing body on stage.

RH:

Yes, the fear of ageing and showing mature bodies on stage is a problem of the Western culture. In Japan, in Kabuki if you are a performer under 40 years old, they don't even take you seriously. From forty, you can start, and you are sixty when they think that something meaningful is beginning to happen now.

In Asia it is more usual to see ageing bodies on stage or even in life: to see old people work. Whereas in our Western culture we send them to retire, force them to stop, make them redundant.

One of my heroes is an elderly German shopkeeper in her late eighties. Ever since I've known her, she opens her shop at 5 o'clock in the morning and works there every day until evening, and would never think of stopping this active life of hers.

In *Si je meurs...* I had to replace a 46 year old dancer, and I auditioned someone younger for the role. I had to realize that the new dancer in her late twenties couldn't fit the role, because she wasn't mature enough. At the end I chose a dancer in her fifties. She was beautiful in that role. And of course when you are a mature dancer you can't do the same thing as a dancer in her twenties, but I don't think this a bad thing.

As I didn't do much dancing before I started my career as a dancer-choreographer in my forties, my body is not that used up. In fact, I can do more than I was able to do many years before, and can carry on dancing...

Endnotes

1   Hoghe, Raimund, *Pina Bausch, Tanztheatergeschichten*, Frankfurt am Main: Surkamp Verlag, 1986.

2   Bausch, Pina, and Ille Chamier and Ulli Weiss, *Setz dich hin und lächle. Tanztheater von Pina Bausch*, Köln: Prometh-Verlag, 1979.

3   Hoghe, Raimund and Ulli Weiss, *Bandoneon – Für was kann Tango alles gut sein?*, München: Luchterhand, 1981.

4   Heiner Müller and Raimund Hoghe and Norbert Servos and Jochen Schmidt and Detlef Erler, *Pina Bausch*, Kilchberg/ Zürich: Edition Stemmle, 1994.

5   Raimund Hoghe, quoted by Thomas Hahn in, Hahn, Thomas, 'Raimund Hoghe, 20 Years, 20 pieces', (translated by Eileen Flügel), on the *Goethe Institut*'s website https://www.goethe.de/en/kul/tut/gen/tan/20363105.html (accessed: 16 September 2015)

PINA BAUSCH BIOGRAPHY

27 July 1940   Philippine Bausch born in Solingen, the third and youngest child of August and Anita Bausch. Her parents ran a small family hotel and restaurant.

1955-1959   Studies dance with Kurt Jooss at the Folkwangschule, Essen. Leaves with a Diploma in Stage Dance and Dance Pedagogy (as well as winning the Folkwang Prize for Achievement in 1958).

1959-1962   Studies a year at the Juilliard School of Music in New York with a scholarship (her teachers include: Antony Tudor and José Limón.) Extends the initial one-year stay to thirty months: works with Paul Sanasardo and Donya Feuer; engaged at the New American Ballet (under Paul Taylor) and at the Metropolitan Opera House Ballet (under Antony Tudor).

1962   Returns to Essen and the Folkwang Hochschule, member of the Folkwang Ballet.

1967   Creates her first choreography for the Folkwang Ballet: *Fragment* to the music of Béla Bartók.

1969   Head of the Folkwang Ballet (until 1973). First prize at the Second International Choreography Competition in Cologne for *Im Wind der Zeit*.

1971   Guest choreography *Aktionen für Tänzer* at the Wuppertaler Bühnen.

1972   Prize for Most Promising Young Artist from the state of North Rhine-Westphalia.

1973   Appointment at the Wuppertaler Bühnen as the Director of Dance; she changes the name of the ballet ensemble to Wuppertaler Tanztheater, later to Tanztheater Wuppertal.

1974   First premiere in Wuppertal: *Fritz* (as part of a triple bill curated by Bausch); choreographs her dance-opera: *Iphigenie auf Tauris* (music: Christoph Willibald Gluck); begins her collaboration with designer Rolf Borzik.

1975   *Orpheus und Eurydike*, dance-opera (music: Christoph Willibald Gluck); *Le Sacre du printemps* (music: Igor Stravinsky).

1976	*Die sieben Todsünden der Kleinbürger/ Fürchtet euch nicht. Tanzabend von Pina Bausch* (music: Kurt Weill, text: Bertolt Brecht).
1977	First Tanztheater Wuppertal tour abroad to Nancy and Vienna; *Blaubart. Beim Anhören einer Tonbandaufnahme von Béla Bartóks Oper "Herzog Blaubarts Burg"* (music: Béla Bartók).
1978	When working on her *Macbeth-Projekt (Er nimmt sie an der Hand und führt sie in das Schloß, die anderen folgen)* for the Schauspielhaus Bochum, Bausch changes her working method and begins posing associative questions to her ensemble of dancers and actors; *Café Müller; Kontakhof.*
1979	Invitation to the Berlin Theatertreffen with *Arien*.
1980	Death of her stage designer and partner Rolf Borzik.
1980	In Chile she meets Ronald Kay, poet and academic, her future partner.
1981	Birth of Bausch and Ronald Kay's son, Rolf Salomon Bausch.
1982	*Nelken*. Plays the role of a blind princess in Fellini's *And the Ship Sails On* (1983).
1983	Appointed as artistic director of the Folkwang Tanzstudio (until her death), and head of the dance department at the Folkwang Hochschule (until 1989).
1984	German Critic's Prize, Berlin; Bessie Award, New York.
1986	*Viktor* – the first 'residency piece', a collaboration with the Teatro Argentina and the City of Rome.
1987	Four-week retrospective in Wuppertal with ten different Tanztheater pieces; Prize of the Dance Critics Society Japan.
1990	Award from the International Theatre Institute on the occasion of World Theatre Day; *Die Klage der Kaiserin*, a dance film directed by Bausch, is released.
1991	Appointed Commandeur de l'Ordre des Arts et des Lettres, France.
1993	UNESCO Picasso Medal.
1994	Retrospective of thirteen pieces from the Tanztheater to celebrate 20 years – as part of the International Dance Festival NRW (North Rhine-Westphalia).

1995	German Dance Prize from the Deutscher Berufsverband für Tanzpädagogik e.V.
1997	Berlin Theatre Prize; Great Cross of the Order of Merit of the Federal Republic of Germany.
1998	*Ein Fest in Wuppertal*: celebrating the 25th anniversary of the Tanztheater Wuppertal; Bambi Award (for culture).
1999	Praemium Imperiale for Theatre and Film, conferred by the Japan Art Association; Honorary Doctorate of the University of Bologna in the fields of visual arts, music and theatre; European Theatre Prize.
2000	Lifetime Achievement Award at the Istanbul Festival; Distinguished Artist Award of the International Society for the Performing Arts (ISPA).
2003	Chevalier de l'Ordre National de la Légion d'Honneur, Paris.
2004	International Dance Festival NRW (North Rhine-Westphalia) under the directorship of Pina Bausch; Nijinsky Award, Monte Carlo.
2005	Golden Mask – Best Foreign Production, Moscow; Honorary Ambassador for Culture and the Arts of the Republic of Korea.
2006	Laurence Olivier Award, London, for *Nelken*; Honorary Doctorate of the Juilliard School, New York; *Vollmond*.
2007	Orden al Mérito Artístico y Cultural 'Pablo Neruda' of the Consejo Nacional de la Cultura y las Artes de Chile, Golden Lion at the Venice Biennale for Lifetime Achievement; Kyoto Prize in the category Art and Philosophy, Kyoto.
2008	International Dance Festival North Rhine-Westphalia under the directorship of Pina Bausch; Goethe Prize from the city of Frankfurt; Honorary Citizen of Wuppertal.
2009	On 30 June Pina Bausch died in Wuppertal; awarded the German theatre prize 'Der Faust' posthumously for her lifetime achievement. Her legacy is over fifty choreographies. She was one of the most significant choreographers of the 20th century.

CONTRIBUTORS

RAIMUND HOGHE was born in Wuppertal and began his career by writing portraits of outsiders and celebrities for the German weekly newspaper *Die Zeit*. These essays were later compiled and published as books.

From 1979 to 1989 Hoghe worked as dramaturg for Pina Bausch's Tanztheater Wuppertal, which became the subject matter for two more books he wrote. His works have been translated into several languages and published in Brazil, France, Germany, Japan, Spain, the United Kingdom and the United States.

Since 1989 he has been creating his own theatre pieces for various dancers and actors. In 1992 he started working with Luca Giacomo Schulte, who has been his artistic collaborator and designer ever since. In 1994 Hoghe produced his first solo for himself, *Meinwärts*, which together with the subsequent *Chambre séparée* (1997) and *Another Dream* (2000) made up a trilogy on the 20th century.

Raimund Hoghe's choreographies have been performed in Europe, North and South America, Asia and Australia, and were awarded with several dance prizes, including the Deutscher Produzentenpreis für Choreografie (2001), the French Prix de la Critique (2006) for *Swan Lake, 4 Acts*. In 2008 critics from the *ballet-tanz* magazine voted him to receive the Dancer of the Year award.

ULLI WEISS (1943–2015) began her career working for Deutsche Lufthansa AG prior to becoming the assistant of Professor Otto Steinert at the Folkwang University for Design in Essen in 1969/70. She studied photography and photojournalism with Steinert in 1971 and graduated in 1976. Her thesis dealt with off-theatre companies in Europe. After completing her degree, Weiss worked as a freelance photographer while pursuing a second degree in Theatre and German Studies. In 1976 she began photographing the rehearsals and performances of the Tanztheater Wuppertal, a work she continued up until her death. Pina Bausch valued her work, as Weiss understood and was able to capture the Tanztheater's aesthetics with her cautious and precise images. Weiss helped shape a visual identity for the Tanztheater for nearly forty years, contributing to almost all of their publications – festival catalogues, books and programmes. Her works include: exhibitions in Milano (*Isadora Duncan, Pina Bausch. Danza dell'anima. Liberazione del Corpo,* 2006 – together with photographer Francesco Carbone) and Frascati (*Pina Bausch, la danza dell'anima,* 2007), and eight books on the artists and work of the Tanztheater Wuppertal. For her contributions towards enriching the culture of Wuppertal, in 2010 Weiss received the Enno und Christa Springmann-Stiftung Award. Ulli Weiss died in Wuppertal in 2015.

PENNY BLACK, after studying drama at Schauspielschule Krauss in Vienna, started her writing career adapting *Yes, My Fuehrer* and *The Galizian Jewess* from the novels by Brigitte Schwaiger for the Edinburgh Festival (1993) and London (1994), both of which won several awards. Since then she has translated, adapted or written over forty plays for a variety of theatres such as the Royal Court, the Gate, the National Theatre, Lyric Hammersmith, Arcola Theatre as well as venues in America and Australia. Her translation of Nobel Laureate Elfriede Jelinek's *Sportsplay* toured the UK during the Olympic year and was chosen as a Cultural Olympic Pop-Up event.

From 2003 to 2005 she served as literary manager of the Gate Theatre. From 2006 to 2012 she was the project co-ordinator for theatre, literature and dance at the Goethe-Institut, London. As a dramaturg Penny has worked widely: most significantly with Broadway producer Annette Niemtzow for White Dog Productions and with Simon McBurney on *Die Zauberfloete* for DNO/ENO.

Penny is published by Oberon Books and Methuen Drama. She is on the board of Company of Angels, a member of The Fence, and is the 2015-2017 Royal Literary Fund Fellow at Oxford Brookes. Since 2016 Penny is serving as President of the Dramaturgs' Network (d'n).

KATALIN TRENCSÉNYI is a London-based dramaturg and researcher. As a freelance dramaturg, Katalin has worked with the National Theatre, the Royal Court Theatre, Deafinitely Theatre, Corali Dance Company, and Company of Angels, among others. As an associate lecturer Katalin has taught at the Royal Academy of Dramatic Art (RADA). She is the author of *Dramaturgy in the Making: A User's Guide for Theatre Practitioners* (Bloomsbury Methuen Drama, 2015), co-editor of *New Dramaturgy: International Perspectives on Theory and Practice* (Bloomsbury Methuen Drama, 2014), and a contributor to *The Routledge Companion to Dramaturgy* (Routledge, 2014). Katalin is co-founder of the Dramaturgs' Network (d'n), served as its President (2010-2012), and currently is sitting on its Advisory Board.

ACKNOWLEDGEMENTS

Raimund Hoghe:

Special thanks to Rudolf Rach at L'Arche and Luca Giacomo Schulte.

Penny Black:

My deep gratitude goes to friend and colleague Katalin Trencsényi for first finding the 1980 original rehearsal diary and then asking me to translate it, starting us off on a fascinating journey. I would like to thank Andrew Walby for saying 'yes', when everything was still in German. And finally a huge thanks to George Spender and all at Oberon Books for their patience and doggedness in pulling everything together to produce this book.

Katalin Trencsényi:

I would like to acknowledge the generous support of the Literary Managers and Dramaturgs' of the Americas' Bly Creative Fellowship Grant that enabled my research for this book. I am particularly grateful to Geoff Proehl for his ongoing support and Cynthia SoRelle for liaising with me throughout, and for Danielle Carroll for the time she spent with grant administration. I would like to say thank you to Beth Blickers for her trust in offering me a slot at the LMDA 30th anniversary conference in New York, where I could test my ideas in a research in action workshop. I am grateful for the generosity of choreographer Arrie Davidson and the creative input of Jess Applebaum who co-lead this workshop with me at Gibney Dance. I thank all the participants of our workshop for their input which helped shape my thinking about dance dramaturgy and the essay in this book.

For my research I am indebted to Anna Lakos at the International Theatre Institut, Budapest, and Tamás Halász and Andrea Varga at the Dance Archives of the National Theatre History Museum and Institut, Budapest, who helped me find some very valuable material for my work. I am also grateful to Frank Hardt at the Pina Bausch Foundation, Wuppertal for his help in giving special access to some of the Pina Bausch Archive's material. Thanks go to Rudi Kliege, Oliver Gladys, Dr. Anne-Kathrin Reif for their help with information, and Nataly

Walter-Bausch for her kind assistance during the working process of this book. I owe thanks to Louie Fleck and everyone at the BAM Hamm Archives and the Performing Arts Library at Lincoln Center, New York. I am also grateful to Mary Kate Connolly at Trinity Laban Conservatoire of Music and Dance for her generosity, dance historian Roman Arndt, choreographer Márta Ladjánszki and translator Adam Versényi for their help.

A big thank you goes to translator Penny Black who was a great partner and a generous friend in this endavour, and George Spender at Oberon Books for his editorial support.

I am indebted to Raimund Hoghe, for his generosity and sharing with me his work, memories, research material, and some precious historical documents and images from the past. I am also grateful for the notes and other help he gave me during my writing and editing of this book. I am also thankful to photographers Detlef Erler and Rosa Frank for their contribution to this book.

I am very grateful to the friends, family and and colleagues who spent much time reading my various manuscripts, offering me feedback: Dan Steward, Nick Tomalin, Peter Eckersall and Bálint Somlyó.

I would also like to say thank you to my family and friends, who in one way or another, enabled my work: Éva Makai, László Trencsényi, Elly Davies, and Lídia Nádori.

Through the inspiration and generosity of Mark Bly, one of North America's trailblazers in the field of theatre dramaturgy, the Literary Managers and Dramaturgs of the Americas launched two innovative granting opportunities to support artists as they continue to chart new territories. The *Bly Creative Fellowship* and *Bly Creative Capacity Grant* are designed to identify and offer significant financial support for exceptional projects. With these grants, the LMDA is committed to facilitating the creative dreams of independent or institutional artists who are defining new ways of conducting dramaturgical activities. The grants are administered by the Literary Managers and Dramaturgs of the Americas

(www.lmda.org).

WWW.OBERONBOOKS.COM

www.ingramcontent.com/pod-product-compliance
Ingram Content Group UK Ltd.
Pitfield, Milton Keynes, MK11 3LW, UK
UKHW031250020325
455689UK00008B/104